ON THE CORNER OF IP AND AMAZON

NAVIGATING TRADEMARK, PATENT, AND COPYRIGHT LAW

MARIO SIMONYAN

This is a work of nonfiction. All of the anecdotes and examples are true, and the author has re-created conversations and details from his memory of them. In order to maintain the anonymity of clients or other parties, some identifying details (including names, locations, or products) have been changed.

LIONCREST
PUBLISHING

On the Corner of IP and Amazon
Navigating Trademark, Patent, and Copyright Law

ISBN 978-1-5445-3943-0 Hardcover
       978-1-5445-3942-3 Paperback
       978-1-5445-3941-6 Ebook

To Leo and Nico,

May you always stay curious.

Contents

Introduction

I'VE ALWAYS BEEN FASCINATED WITH THE BUSINESS OF importing and exporting. When I was an elementary school student (and while many of my contemporaries were playing Little League or attending Cub Scout meetings) I was fantasizing about importing enough Lamborghinis so that I could eventually own that kind of fantasy sports car.

As a law student, I watched as many of my classmates took jobs ranging from waiting tables and loading UPS trucks to clerking for attorneys or working as paralegals to pay for tuition. With all of our course requirements, I knew I didn't have time for that kind of thing. Besides, I'd also always known that I would prefer to start my own business instead of working for someone else.

This was right when Amazon's Fulfillment by Amazon (FBA) program was really taking off: launched in 2006, the program allows third-party sellers to store their products with Amazon; the company also takes care of packing, shipping, and customer service on behalf of those sellers. FBA was a game changer, and customers began flocking to the site in search of convenient ways to buy everything from CDs to PlayStations. I saw a real opportunity in this and began watching YouTube instructional videos on how to launch a successful online business. That's when everything clicked.

To this day, I can't remember if I borrowed against one of my student loans or maxed out one of my credit cards, but I do know that I used that money to order a thousand units of a combination avocado slicer and pit remover—not because I have an obsessive interest in making guacamole, but rather, because I knew that women made up a particularly strong demographic of Amazon shoppers, and the women in my life really enjoy cooking and experimenting with new kitchen gadgets.

The hunch paid off. In no time, my new Amazon storefront had sold out of all the avocado slicers. I ordered another thousand, and they soon went as well. I added a second product—a strawberry stem remover—and they sold out too. Not long after, I added a cutting board and chef's knife, along with a magnetic strip on which to hang it and other knives. They sold out as well, and I was feeling confident I'd mastered the Amazon Marketplace.

A little too confident, as it turned out.

On a whim, I ordered a shipping container of artificial grass from China. Five massive rolls arrived, and I immediately realized there was no easy way I was going to be able to sell it. The rolls of artificial grass languished in their container, while I stewed about my hubris, dismayed that I would never be able to unload the shipment.

One morning as I was drinking my coffee, an idea dawned on me: *what if we cut up the artificial turf and make doormats?* I hired a few people from one of the big-box hardware stores to size and cut the.mats.

The first go-round was a total mess: the edges weren't cut straight, and many of the mats had fraying or uneven edges. But we kept at it. We ordered some cut-rate black-and-white labels; we purchased poly bags in which to ship the rolled-up mats; I took some amateurish photos of it all and put it on Amazon. Guess what? *They* ended up taking off too. We were the first company to sell these mats, and there was a definite demand. We negotiated with a manufacturer who supplied artificial turf to professional soccer stadiums around the world and secured a shipment of our own specially cut design. At the time, I didn't make much of the turf representative's repeated questions about whether or not I really wanted to do this. In hindsight, that was clearly a mistake. It never occurred to me to protect my product with any kind of intellectual property (IP) rights, whether it was a design patent or trademark for the mat or a copyright for our advertising language and other branding materials. Other online sellers noticed our success, and they soon began producing their own mats as well, with no legal consequences. Our corner of the market quickly disappeared.

As an Amazon sellers' lawyer, a former Amazon seller, and now the founder of ESQgo®, a successful intellectual property law firm, I still see this kind of issue again and again.

And frankly, those clients are the lucky ones. Others have found their listings removed from the site, their accounts suspended, their inventory destroyed, or their businesses kicked off the site entirely. That's because, in a lot of ways, Amazon is its own sovereign nation, complete with its own laws and legal processes. To be successful there, you have to understand those laws as well as how to participate in the court of Amazon. You also need to understand what business models work for online sales and why. To navigate it all successfully takes a level of business maturity as well as knowing when you need to consult an attorney specializing in intellectual property who can help you determine what to protect, when to establish those protections, and how.

Amazon is the wild, wild west: a place where villains wearing black hats have become very skilled at playing dirty and using tactics to undermine and even ruin their competition. They've figured out how to get your Amazon products and pages suspended, and they'll go to dramatic ends to make sure that's what happens. The more successful you are there, the more issues you are going to have with competitors who refuse to play fair.

To further complicate matters, Amazon can be a black box where information is concerned, so knowing what you have access to and what you can control is also a challenge. The company's policies are constantly evolving and changing, which can make it difficult for sellers to know how best to navigate the space and what options they have available to them should they need to take action, including seeking arbitration. The fact of the matter is that the deck is already stacked against you as soon as you find yourself in a dispute about your Amazon business. Arbitration can be expensive and time consuming, drawn out for months or even years, all while your account is suspended and your business is losing money.

On the Corner of IP and Amazon: Navigating Trademark, Patent, and Copyright Law provides companies and private sellers with a practical guidebook for managing intellectual property concerns in an online marketplace. To be clear: this book isn't going to tell you how to sell on Amazon or provide any tricks to that effect. It also will not provide a complete education on intellectual property. What it will do is teach you the essential basics of IP: how IP should (and shouldn't) be used, what to keep in mind when creating or marketing a new product, how to identify when IP is being used against you incorrectly, and what you need to know to have an intelligent conversation with a qualified IP attorney.

In the chapters that follow, I'll provide some background on the evolution of the e-commerce marketplace and how best to monetize intellectual property. I'll explain the difference between copyrights, trademarks, and patents, along with how and when to employ all three to best protect your products and business. I'll also provide a primer on what is unique about Amazon law and how your competitors are exploiting that law to their own advantage. Finally, I'll discuss the options and resources available to you, should you find yourselves faced with a suspension or another type of legal snag.

As an attorney specializing in these kinds of cases, I have dedicated my professional career to helping clients navigate Amazon's legal system and the unique challenges it poses. My legal firm, ESQgo®, has been successfully serving the needs of entrepreneurs and businesses around the world and in over thirty-five different countries. From small mom-and-pop establishments to brands earning over $900 million in annual revenue, we've helped clients navigate the unique challenges associated with e-commerce, whether that means registering for intellectual property protections or pursuing an infringement claim.

Our firm's proprietary Synthetic Arbitration® process provides clients with a fast, affordable, and effective resolution process that combines creative problem-solving and aggressive advocacy. And it works. SynArb® has provided over 250 of our clients with swift and satisfactory solutions that have them back on Amazon and successfully earning revenue. As a former Amazon seller who has built and sold two seven-figure businesses, I've learned firsthand what works, where the pitfalls lie, and how to avoid them.

After reading this book, you will too.

CHAPTER 1

The Digital Marketplace

AMAZON FOUNDER JEFF BEZOS ALWAYS INTENDED TO CREATE a company that could sell virtually anything to anyone. Formally trained as a computer scientist and electrical engineer, Bezos spent nearly a decade working in a New York financial firm. But in the early 1990s, he correctly predicted that the rise of the internet would revolutionize retail purchasing, and he committed to becoming a part of that revolution.

By 1994, Bezos had relocated to Washington State and launched a beta version of Amazon: dubbed by Bezos "the world's largest bookstore," it sold only that one product and, at least initially, used Bezos's garage as its headquarters and distribution center. However, Bezos had always envisioned his new startup as one that would grow rapidly, both in terms of size and sales, and also in the variety of products sold. By 1999, Amazon was selling everything from toys and electronics to tools and music. A year later, it had introduced a platform that allowed other companies and individuals to sell their products at the site as well.

One of the most significant shifts for the company was adopting Fulfillment by Amazon (FBA) in 2006. FBA allows third-party sellers to utilize Amazon's distribution centers and sophisticated fulfillment models in order to route products to customers. For many merchants, particularly individuals and small companies, this service allows them to expedite delivery by capitalizing on Amazon's hundreds of fulfillment centers spread out across the globe; it also codifies otherwise volatile shipping expenses and ensures that sellers always pay the same flat fee. Finally, FBA allows sellers to avoid the hassles associated with returns, customer service, and inventory accounting.

Innovations such as FBA quickly made Amazon a trusted site, where buyers knew they could return items for virtually any reason whatsoever. The popularity of this digital marketplace is undoubtedly what has brought so many sellers to it, and the allure of being part of a virtual monopoly is undeniably difficult to resist. Take the case of David Barnett, founder of PopSockets—those round, knob-like grips that can be attached to the back of a smartphone. After Amazon began selling the grips for a lower price and demanding that PopSockets pay for the lost margin, Barnett severed his relationship with the digital giant. A year later, Barnett was back selling on Amazon. Why? Because he estimates his company lost approximately $10 million in revenue for the twelve months it did not list products on Amazon.

The onset of COVID-19 only accelerated Amazon's already robust sales. With stay-at-home orders not only across the country but also around the world, shoppers radically changed their habits from in-store to online purchasing. A recent *New York Times* study found that Amazon boasted a 220 percent profit increase during the first year of the pandemic; meanwhile, merchant revenue increased 64 percent, or $23.7 billion. Not only did the pandemic have a strong impact on Amazon sales, but it also widened the entire e-commerce marketplace, from giant corporations like Walmart to individual artisans on Etsy.com. As pandemic restrictions began to lift, those trends continued. Today, market watchers predict that this growth in e-commerce will continue long after COVID-19 is just an unfortunate memory: again and again, customers are demonstrating that they continue to prefer the convenience of online sales.

Today, there are over six million sellers on Amazon—more than double the number there were in 2017. Roughly ten thousand of those sellers garner over $1 million annually. Here in the US, Amazon has 2.3 million active, third-party sellers (those who are independent from Amazon but use the site as a marketplace for their goods). About 850,000 of them, or roughly 37 percent, rely on Amazon as their sole source of income. Most use FBA for their inventory management.

Common E-commerce Sales Models

In general, Amazon sellers fall into one of three groups: arbitrage, wholesale, and private- (or white-) label sellers.

Arbitrage sellers are those who purchase a limited amount of a product at one price from a major retailer and then sell it on Amazon at another. These sellers might, for instance, see that a particular brand of ballpoint pens is on sale at a store like Staples and purchase dozens of boxes at that reduced price, only to then turn around and sell those pens at a full or even an inflated price on Amazon.

A questionable but nevertheless common variation on arbitrage is *drop shipping:* under this model, a seller will list an item at its full price on Amazon while combing other sites for better deals. For instance, that seller may see that a bottle of a particular brand of perfume regularly retails at Amazon for $100 while, at the same time, a department store like Macy's is featuring it on sale for $50. Instead of buying up a hundred or more bottles of the discounted perfume at Macy's, the seller will wait until a customer places an order at their Amazon marketplace and only then place an order for a bottle of the perfume at Macy's. When placing that order, the seller will then simply insert the unwitting Amazon customer's name and address as the intended recipient when checking out at the other retailer—such as Macy's. Both Amazon and Walmart prohibit this sort of drop shipping: too often, sellers find that the product is no longer available *after* they've already sold the item and must then cancel the order. Other times, even when the item is available, the customer experiences delays in receiving it, or the product is not shipped with the same care and quality branded packaging as one can expect with a company like Amazon. Still other times, a customer is just confused by the delivery they placed on Amazon arriving in a Macy's packaging, and might refuse or return it. An acquaintance of mine once ordered a set of knives on Amazon. When a large box from Walmart arrived with an unknown person's name and address listed as the sender, the acquaintance assumed it was an error on the part of the delivery company and returned the box unopened, never guessing that her knives were enclosed.

A second variation on this model is known as *gray market goods*, which are products that are intended to be sold in one country but wind up in another. For instance, I might purchase vitamins in Mexico at a discounted price and then sell them to United States customers. In Chapter 5 of this book, we'll take a much closer look at this model, why it can be problematic, and what's at stake, both for the sellers who employ it and the buyers who are the unsuspecting recipients of the practice.

One of the most common approaches to e-commerce is *wholesale* selling. Unlike arbitrage sellers, who are often individual people working out of their home and spending relatively little up-front capital on products and infrastructure, *wholesale* sellers must be willing to make a real investment on both of these fronts: instead of buying a few dozen pens from a big-box store, wholesale sellers are more likely buying tens of thousands of boxes, which in turn require dedicated warehouse space, a sustained relationship with a wholesaler, and a business model that will ensure they are able to resell the items they purchased in bulk (and often at a considerable up-front cost). Wholesale sellers also face additional Amazon-imposed hurdles to their businesses, including securing invoices from Amazon-verified wholesalers.

The final sales model is known as *private label*, in which a seller builds upon the wholesale model but, instead of purchasing ten thousand brand-name pens, the seller contracts with a manufacturer to make a product of their own—under their own brand name. These sellers might, for instance, put their own logo on a pen or make other small adjustments like changing the cap or the shade of ink. In addition to the legal, logistical, and financial considerations of the wholesale market, private label sales come with additional complications, including safety and compliance considerations, particularly if their products are produced overseas. They must also assume the risk and potential liability if their products either fail to comply with US safety standards or they are defective. In either case, a *private label* seller can't just return these items to the manufacturer, as you can in a wholesale relationship. Instead, they might find themselves stuck with one hundred thousand leaking pens, a lot of ink on their hands, and a series of negative customer reviews on Amazon. If their products infringe upon another seller's patents or trademarks, they might also find themselves with an expensive lawsuit to deal with.

A variation on the private label sales model is what I like to call *private label 2.0.* When Amazon first opened its marketplace to third-party merchants, there was plenty of room for private label sellers, even if they were offering niche items like a strawberry destemmer. However, as the marketplace has proliferated and become increasingly congested, simply adding a unique logo or tiny tweak to an existing product is often no longer enough to distinguish yourself from other sellers. Consequently, many sellers are resorting to *private label 2.0.* Under this model, entrepreneurs must find additional ways to distinguish themselves from the competition: instead of just selling a strawberry destemmer or avocado pitter, they might instead offer one gadget that does both. The innovation of this combined pitter and destemmer might succeed in luring customers their way, but only if they've also protected the new product with the appropriate intellectual property safeguards so that copycat sellers aren't soon listing the same gadget as well.

Choosing the right business model is essential to your success as a digital seller. Each requires a familiarity with intellectual property law and how best you can protect your brand and the products you sell. Whether it's a copyright, trademark, or patent, the right protection will not only help ensure that you corner the market on current sales, it can also increase future revenue and substantially increase your company's entire business valuation.

CHAPTER 2

Trademarks

IN 2010, A LANDMARK SCHOLARLY STUDY DEMONSTRATED what many parents have long suspected: young children become savvy brand consumers even long before they can read. This particular study, which was published in the journal *Psychology and Marketing,* surveyed kids aged three to five years old and found that nearly all of them could identify logos like Coca-Cola's iconic script or Disney's stylized castle. Even more surprising was the fact that these same children could also recognize logos for companies that had no obvious connection to that age demographic: corporations like Nike, Toyota, and Shell were all readily recognizable to these preschoolers. Meanwhile, other popular brand images, like Ronald McDonald or Wendy, were more recognizable to the children than recent presidents.

What that academic study also confirmed is just how valuable a company's brand can be, regardless of whether it represents a Fortune 500 corporation or a small mom-and-pop store. The sheer value of a business's brand is why big entities spend millions of dollars on design elements like their company logo (British Petroleum or BP, for instance, famously spent $211 million on their sunflower-inspired logo back in 2008). It's also why every company or business, no matter how large or small, should protect their brand with appropriate trademarks.

Simply put, a trademark is a legal protection for the images, words, or phrases that identify your brand, products, or services. As such, a trademark can protect anything from NBC's multicolored peacock to the particular shade of blue made famous by Tiffany's blue jewelry boxes: "robin's-egg blue." There are several different types of trademarks to consider. Standard character trademarks are for particular words unique to your brand. Often, these are brand or company names, like *Twitter* or *Domino's*; they can also be phrases like

Nike's *Just Do It*® or Wheaties' *The Breakfast of Champions*®. The standard character trademark protects only the actual words themselves—not how they appear in print or on a computer screen. Special form trademarks, on the other hand, protect the style and design of a brand, such as Amazon's orange smiling arrow, Nike's swoosh, or McDonald's golden arches. More ephemeral design elements, such as the red-and-white interior of In-N-Out Burger or even the angled exterior facade of a Walgreens, are also eligible for trademark protections, using a concept known as *trade dress*. If you've ever walked into a Starbucks, you can probably picture what I'm talking about: the wood paneling, high-top chairs, the stand of travel mugs for purchase, the green of the baristas' aprons, and even the use of Italian for the drink sizes all make it very clear what coffee chain you are visiting. Elements included under trade dress protection can include anything from a particular color, a scent (Hasbro actually trademarked the smell of Play-Doh), or a sound, like the roar of the MGM lion heard at the start of their films. Trade dress characteristics can also include textures, graphics, and moving images.

A successful company will go to great lengths to protect its trademarks. Try selling women's shoes with a red sole, and you are undoubtedly going to hear from Christian Louboutin's attorneys. Include the sound of a low-pitched gong in a commercial for your new Mexican restaurant, and Taco Bell is probably going to come after you. Why? Because both of those elements are trademarked. So is the cherry scent added to a specific brand of high-performance automobile lubricant and the bubble-gum aroma someone thought to put in the soles of a specific brand of flip-flops. Knowing what to trademark and how will make your selling experience on Amazon and other digital marketplaces that much more successful.

Trademarks also exist to protect the reputation of your brand, even if your business is brand new. I always advise my clients that applying for a trademark is one of the first and most foundational steps in creating a successful business. You can spend hundreds of hours and tens of thousands of dollars coming up with the perfect name for your new company or product. But if you don't also take the time to protect that brand, you may soon find that competitors have stolen it and gotten away scot-free. Taking the time to build your company's brand and reputation can take years and considerable expense. Without a trademark process as part of that work, you may discover the hard way that someone else already has claim to your name or brand identity, forcing you to undergo an expensive rebrand that will also undoubtedly cost you customer and sales opportunities.

Without trademarks, anyone could sell computers featuring a bitten apple or raise money for disaster relief with a red cross. Trademarks are particularly important on digital marketplaces, where brand recognition may be the only thing separating you from your competition.

Regardless of whether you are seeking trademark or trade dress protections, much of the application process is exactly the same. Navigating that process successfully can save your company time and money.

The Trademark Application Process

Trademarks are issued and enforced by the United States Patent and Trademark Office (USPTO), an agency located within the Department of Commerce and with a dedicated mission of promoting industrial and technological progress in the US. Companies are not required to retain an intellectual property attorney to apply for a trademark, unless they are a foreign entity. That said, hiring qualified representation offers several notable benefits. Not only can the attorney conduct clearance searches on your behalf, they can also ensure that your application is correctly prepared and filed, and they can advocate on your behalf, should you encounter a snag with the USPTO.

Filing a successful trademark application begins with knowing what type of application to file. There are two separate categories for a trademark application. The first is known as *use in commerce*, which is to say your goods or services are currently in interstate commerce. Say, for instance, that you have just launched a new business selling artisanal soaps. If you are already selling your soap from one state to another or are taking international orders, you are engaged in interstate commerce. The second type of application is known as *intent to use*. This application is earmarked for trademarks not yet used in commerce, but for which the owner has a good-faith intention of doing so in the future. The benefit of applying for this type of trademark is that it allows you to seek protections for your product or service early in the process and, in doing so, potentially avoid conflicts with other new products deemed confusingly similar by the USPTO.

A successful *intent to use* trademark application requires a sworn statement attesting to your bona fide (or *good faith*) intention to use the trademark in commerce. A *use in commerce* application, on the other hand, must include proof that your company is already actively using your product or service. This could include a picture with your brand name on the product or a screenshot of your website showing your brand name and the particular product; in either case, one of these specimens would need to be included with your application. Historically, the USPTO's application review process was about three months for an examining attorney to review the application. However, over the past couple of years, a rapid rise in applications has extended that time to as many as seven months.

Once the USPTO has considered an application, that office will usually take one of several actions: ideally, they will approve the application. In that instance, the USPTO will then publish your application, which gives the public thirty days to contest its approval. If no one does, then the application process will be considered complete, and a trademark will be registered.

What follows are three examples of Certificates of Registration issued by the USPTO. In these examples, you'll see that each trademark has an individual serial and registration number. The serial number is assigned during the application process and remains unique to the trademark, whether or not it is approved by the USPTO. The registration number is only provided by the USPTO upon registration. Trademarks are also distinguished as within either *product* or *service* categories—otherwise known as an International Class, and this designation must be made as part of the application process.

United States of America
United States Patent and Trademark Office

MATCHIMAL

Reg. No. 6,343,210

Registered May 04, 2021

Int. Cl.: 28

Trademark

Principal Register

GuruEcom, LLC (CALIFORNIA LIMITED LIABILITY COMPANY)
Unit 12
7341 Fulton Avenue
North Hollywood, CALIFORNIA 91605

CLASS 28: Puzzles

FIRST USE 1-5-2021; IN COMMERCE 2-12-2021

THE MARK CONSISTS OF STANDARD CHARACTERS WITHOUT CLAIM TO ANY PARTICULAR FONT STYLE, SIZE OR COLOR

SER. NO. 88-859,192, FILED 04-03-2020

Performing the Functions and Duties of the
Under Secretary of Commerce for Intellectual Property and
Director of the United States Patent and Trademark Office

United States of America
United States Patent and Trademark Office

ESQGO

Reg. No. 5,872,459

Registered Oct. 01, 2019

Int. Cl.: 45

Service Mark

Principal Register

ESQGO, PC (CALIFORNIA CORPORATION)
303 North Glenoaks Blvd., Suite 200
Burbank, CALIFORNIA 91502

CLASS 45: Providing legal services in the field of intellectual property law and e-commerce law

FIRST USE 5-1-2018; IN COMMERCE 5-25-2018

THE MARK CONSISTS OF STANDARD CHARACTERS WITHOUT CLAIM TO ANY PARTICULAR FONT STYLE, SIZE OR COLOR

SER. NO. 88-340,483, FILED 03-14-2019

Director of the United States
Patent and Trademark Office

United States of America
United States Patent and Trademark Office

Reg. No. 6,541,463

Registered Oct. 26, 2021

Int. Cl.: 21

Trademark

Supplemental Register

Rise8 Studios LLC (NEVADA LIMITED LIABILITY COMPANY)
2020.00429
1000 N Green Valley Pkwy, #440-239
Henderson, NEVADA 89074

CLASS 21: Spatulas for kitchen use, Cooking Spoons and Forks, Serving Spoons and Forks, Wooden Cooking Spoons and Forks

FIRST USE 9-20-2016; IN COMMERCE 9-20-2016

The mark consists of a three-dimensional configuration of a kitchen utensil handle that is shaped like the neck and head of an electric guitar. The elements shown in dotted lines show the placement of the mark on the utensil and not part of the mark.

SER. NO. 90-482,934, FILED P.R. 01-22-2021; AM. S.R. 08-20-2021

Performing the Functions and Duties of the
Under Secretary of Commerce for Intellectual Property and
Director of the United States Patent and Trademark Office

As you can see from these examples, a trademark can be issued for a company's name (such as my firm, ESQgo®) or for a distinctive shape, such as the guitar spatula. The latter is an example of *trade dress,* which is to say that what is actually being protected is the three-dimensional configuration of the product.

Interestingly, in the example of the guitar spatula, my client was initially denied a trademark by the USPTO because they were unable to prove that no one else was using that specific design. Instead, they were told they would need to wait a certain number of years to establish that the design was, in fact, unique to their company. In that case, we asked for permission to amend our client's application from the principal trademark registry to the *supplemental registry.* The USPTO's supplemental registry records trademarks that are not yet considered "distinctive," and while they do not receive all of the legal protections of the principal registry, this step can help to establish your brand or product's primacy, should someone attempt to register a similar product while your trademark is pending the potential of acquiring distinctiveness. Holders who have a trademark in the supplemental registry and can demonstrate five years of continuous use may apply for inclusion in the principal registry based on a legal concept known as "secondary meaning." For example, Bank of America, Dollar Shave Club, and Lowe's were initially on the supplement registry due to being geographic, descriptive, and a surname, respectively.

When considering a trademark application, another action the USPTO might take is known as an issuance of an *office action*. Common reasons for an office action include a mistake or typo in the application materials (for instance, you list your address as St. Louis, MI instead of St. Louis, MO). More substantive office actions can arise if your application is found to be *confusingly similar* to another pending or registered trademark, which is what occurred in the case of one of my clients, Baby Trio.

Prior to hiring my firm, Baby Trio had been reliably netting about $2 million annually selling foldable baby bathtubs on Amazon. When its founders initially launched the company, they did so without going through the trademark process. As their folding bathtubs began to rise in popularity, the company hired a law firm that failed to conduct a thorough search to see if any existing trademarks might be in conflict with the one for which Baby Trio was applying. As a result of this error, Baby Trio had no idea that an existing brand was already selling products for infants under the name *Baby Tree*.

The USPTO discovered this would-be rival and sent a notification to Baby Trio that the trademark application they had filed to protect their name could not be approved because it was too similar to Baby Tree's. In other words, the USPTO had deemed it likely that a consumer searching for a product such as that foldable bathtub might go looking for one of the two companies and accidentally select the other, thinking they'd found their intended brand. The USPTO reserves this designation of "confusingly similar" for companies selling the same or similar type of goods or services.

Once the USPTO makes the determination that two brands or products are confusingly similar, an applicant is faced with several equally undesirable choices. First, they could approach the existing company and ask for permission to retain their name. In the dog-eat-dog world of e-commerce, you might occasionally be lucky enough to find a company generous enough to allow you to impinge upon their brand identity, but that eventuality is highly unlikely. The second option would be to change the name of their company in order to distinguish themselves from their competitor. This option is both a costly and onerous process, which can include having to register for a new domain name, revising catalog and marketing materials, and potentially losing a client base that only knows to find you by your original name. The third option is to contest the USPTO decision by drafting a series of arguments in response to the USPTO office's actions, that attempt to prove the two names are not confusingly similar. That battle is almost always an uphill one, and it can quickly become both time consuming and expensive. The fourth option is to initiate a Cancellation Proceeding before the USPTO's Trademark Trial and Appeals Board (TTAB) to invalidate the "confusingly similar" trademark on one of the following grounds:

- fraud upon the USPTO,
- abandonment or non-use,
- generic or merely descriptive,
- failure to function as a trademark,
- trademark dilution, or
- lacked bona fide intent to use

This TTAB process is a legal proceeding with complaints, discovery, and briefs; it can often cost between $50,000–$70,000 to litigate, and it comes with no guarantee of success.

In short, for a company with a bottom line like Baby Trio's, there was simply no way to avoid real financial hardship. In the end, they got lucky: after initiating a TTAB proceeding, we were able to persuade Baby Tree to let Baby Trio keep its company name, so long as the latter restricted the products they sold to that foldable bathtub. It wasn't a perfect compromise, but in the world of IP law, it was as good as we could have hoped for.

What makes this anecdote a particularly painful one is the fact that the situation was completely avoidable. Had the founders of Baby Trio sought out a qualified intellectual property attorney early in their branding process, they would have been counseled to pay the modest fee (usually less than $1,000) needed to conduct a trademark clearance search, which not only locates any "confusingly similar" trademarks, but also identifies other conflicts, such as names that sound the same (even if they are spelled differently) or words that are synonymous with crucial language in your brand name or slogans. The trademark search would have discovered that the USPTO most likely would have issued an office action stating that their company name was confusingly similar to Baby Tree, particularly given the nature of the products sold by both companies. At that point, Baby Trio would have had to decide if they wanted to fight the office action. In the event that they chose that course of action, we would have worked together to draft arguments about why the decision was wrong and their name was *not* confusingly similar to Baby Tree. But given how nascent their company was, it probably would have been easiest simply to settle upon a different and more distinct name for their business.

A good IP lawyer also would have advised the founders of Baby Trio to make their trademark application as broad as possible. A trademark that describes its goods as a "folding bathtub" is very specific, which means it offers your potential competitors a greater playing field on which to sell their own products. If, on the other hand, a company like Baby Trio filed a trademark application for "bathtubs, bathtub enclosures, and shower trays," they would broaden the scope of their own protections and make it that much more difficult for their competitors to distinguish their potential products.

In other words, the broader the trademark, the wider the barricade you build around your own brand.

When it comes to "confusingly similar" conflicts, some trademark applicants may have an ace up their sleeve if it turns out that they began interstate commerce before their competitor. This concept is known as *priority of use*. In other words, trademark law gives preference to companies or individuals who first use a trademark, even if they failed to register that trademark or file an application. To make that case, you must be able to prove that you were the first to enter into interstate commerce with the trademarked product or service. If your brand has priority of use, but a competitor has filed a USPTO trademark before you, you may still be able to obtain a trademark registration and invalidate the trademark application filed before you. However, it is very likely that you would need to start a legal proceeding before the Trademark Trial and Appeal Board (TTAB) to invalidate or cancel the aforementioned trademark. Costs associated with such a proceeding can easily exceed $50,000, which is why I always caution companies to think about the impact of those fees and whether a more affordable option might be available.

How and Why Trademarks Help

As identifiable to most people as McDonald's golden arches or Nike's swoosh are the standard trademark symbols: that small ® indicating a registered trademark or the superscript ™ indicating that the mark owners intend to use this mark as a trademark. The latter can even be used on brand names or logos *before* the application has been submitted. Nevertheless, common law rights afford you some protection from the moment you begin using the material you wish to trademark.

There are many other benefits to trademarks. Most notably, they put your competitors on notice that you reserve the right to use a logo or brand, or that a product is yours. As we saw in the Baby Trio example, it behooves businesses to hire a good IP attorney from the outset. That lawyer will undoubtedly conduct a thorough trademark search, which will uncover what has already been protected. What that lawyer is looking for is basically your right and left limits. In the case of Baby Tree, for instance, an IP attorney may determine that there is already a trademark on foldable baby bathtubs, but not on inflatable baby bathtubs. Or perhaps that attorney will find that, while baby bathtubs are protected, doggy bathtubs are not. That kind of search will give you a good indication of what your options are, not just for protecting your particular item or brand, but also for protecting your places for expansion. If that lawyer finds that your chosen brand or product is already protected, they may advise you to consider other options as well.

The other benefit a trademark offers is that it grants you priority with the USPTO. Let's go back to the hypothetical soap example. Say you decide to name your company ZAPPY ZOAPS, and you file the trademark application accordingly. Unbeknownst to you, another company is already in existence with the name SAPPY SOAPS. That competitor has been selling soap for several years, but only just now decided to trademark their name. As I explained earlier, they could argue priority of use and attempt to override your trademark application, but you have priority in the application process because you were first to file. For SAPPY SOAPS to prevail, they would have to bring their case to the Trademark Trial and Appeal Board in an attempt to override your application —a potentially costly and lengthy process that many small businesses just can't afford to pursue.

A corollary benefit would be the cost of enforcing a trademark. If you are in possession of a trademark certificate, a simple correspondence notifying a competitor or would-be competitor of your trademark is often all it takes to persuade them to abandon the brand or product; as any good IP attorney will tell you, that certificate is legitimate evidence difficult to combat in court.

Pointing out its mere existence is far easier (and thus cheaper) than attempting to prove that you have prior use considerations or amassing a case as to why the trademark should be handed over to you. Should you find that your trademark has been infringed upon, you can also seek enhanced damages in a court of law. These are statutory amounts dictated by the courts that compensate trademark holders for damages they may have incurred. Because these sums are fixed, trademark holders do not need to worry about accounting for the total damages they incurred, nor are they required to go through the lengthy and often costly process of locating and securing expert witnesses who testify on their behalf about the estimated damages. Should someone infringing upon their trademark continue to do so, a trademark holder may also qualify for treble, or triple the damages, if that holder is able to prove that a party has intentionally continued to infringe upon their trademark.

It's also worth noting that US courts do not require a complainant to hold a trademark registration in order to claim trademark infringement. That said, a trademark is far from an ironclad protection, especially in its early years. I often advise my clients to think of it as a newborn baby: fragile to the point of vulnerability for its first several years. That's because people can continue to contest it for the first five years. After that time, the USPTO will require you to file additional documents attesting to the fact that it has been in use for those five years. At that point, your trademark will become incontestable unless it is proven that that trademark was obtained by fraud, was abandoned, or has become generic, a difficult bar to meet.

Brand Registry: Amazon's Version of the Trademark

Since its founding in 1994, Amazon has become a veritable country unto itself, complete with its own constitution, laws, and now, its own court system. To that end, they've established their own protections, including where intellectual property matters are concerned. One of the most obvious examples is Amazon's *Brand Registry*.

Launched in 2017, Amazon's Brand Registry uses machine learning and data algorithms to help sellers protect their brand—and the products they sell. It also gives sellers greater control over how their products are listed on the site. That includes adding video and stylized images to your product page, along with graphics and diagrams, all of which can create great exposure and increase sales.

Today, more than five hundred thousand brands in over twenty countries are currently registered in service, and Amazon promises 24/7 support of any IP infringement on those registered brands. To be eligible for these protections, you must either have a registered trademark or an application for one pending. The inclusion of pending applications is a huge boon for new sellers: because the USPTO trademark approval process can take a year—or more—it's great to know that Amazon can provide some protection in the meantime.

Brand Registry further empowers sellers awaiting word from the USPTO in some unexpected ways. Say, for instance, that

I am an Amazon seller who wants to protect my new line of heated coffee mugs that plug into a car's USB port. I've filed for a trademark with the USPTO. I'm given my unique serial number and told that it could be nine months or more before my application is registered. That's a long time to wait, especially if I have a warehouse of mugs waiting to be sold. But I also know that putting them on the digital marketplace without any protections could jeopardize my future as a coffee mug seller. One option I have is to take my USPTO serial number and enroll with Amazon Brand Registry. Doing so not only allows me to use Amazon's automated protections to more quickly report violations and have those listings removed, but I can then also utilize enhanced services like Amazon's *Project Zero*, which provides automated protections by using information about your product to block counterfeits before they even enter the marketplace.

An important word of caution about Amazon's Brand Registry: because an official USPTO trademark is not required to enroll, there are some bad actors who have found ways to exploit this service. If I were a nefarious competitor, I could file for a bogus trademark I know that I'll never get. But until that application is rejected, I will still have a USPTO serial number that looks legitimate to Amazon's AI algorithms. So if I am a bad actor, there's nothing preventing me from gaining Amazon protections to which I have no legitimate rights and using them to create legal hassles for truly legitimate sellers. We'll talk more about these types of scams, known as "black hat tactics," in Chapter 6.

Distinguishing Your Brand

One of my favorite stories of a successful trademark becoming the emblem of an entire brand is that of Burberry, the British luxury label made famous by its tan, black, and red checkered pattern. The company was founded in the late 1800s but didn't become truly successful for another fifty years. During the interim, its full-length raincoats became an official part of the British military uniform (hence the name "trench coat"). After World War I, veterans brought home their coats, which had held up remarkably well on the Western Front. Soon, it seemed like all of England wanted one. Beginning in the 1920s, Burberry began lining its coats with that signature Scottish tartan check. By the 1960s, it had become one of the most sought-after fashion elements around the world. That tartan—known as the Burberry House check—has been featured on luggage and handbags, hats and scarves, golf shirts and baby strollers. Today, the Burberry brand is valued at approximately $5.2 billion—all because of their trademarked tartan.

Similar stories can be told about John Deere's special green and yellow paint, or even the melted red wax atop each bottle of Maker's Mark bourbon. If you haven't already done so, now is a great time to ask yourself what design elements might become a part of your winning brand. Consider my clients Baby Trio. They might choose a particular shade and combination of pink and green as their brand colors. That design could be trademarked. So too could a particular sound effect, such as a baby's happy coo paired with the splash of water in a tub. Perhaps Baby Trio decided to have their tubs infused with a lavender scent. That, too, could be trademarked. Then again, maybe there's something essential about the shape or folding mechanisms of the bathtub itself that could be trademarked. And why not? One reason Lamborghinis have the immense culture cache that they do is because of their scissor doors, which are also trademarked.

The very ease and convenience of selling on Amazon is precisely why you need to do everything you can to create and protect your brand's trademarks. More than perhaps any other commercial platform, Amazon has forced businesses large and small to evolve rapidly and become increasingly creative. If I'm successful selling baby bathtubs or sustainable soap or even just ballpoint pens, you can guarantee that other would-be merchants are going to look to capitalize on that success. The more you have protected your brand with appropriate trademarks, the more you've afforded yourself the kind of competitive advantage needed to survive—and prosper—within the Amazon Marketplace and beyond. That also includes multiple IP registrations that cover every possible aspect of your brand and the products you sell. But remember: although a trademark is powerful, it is still only one intellectual property protection. That's why understanding other protections, including copyrights, is so important for your business's success.

CHAPTER 3

Copyrights

Moby Dick.

Don't Stop Believing.

The Matrix.

'Twas the Night before Christmas.

One World Trade Center.

WHAT DO ALL OF THESE WORKS HAVE IN COMMON? THEY'VE all been copyrighted. Whereas trademarks are best considered as brand names and logos, copyrights often apply to books, music, movies, poems, and architecture. In legal terminology, copyrights protect the expression of an idea that has been fixed in a tangible medium of expression. What that means is that you can't protect a thought or a vision for a work, but once you've put that work on paper (or even in a Google Doc), it has become eligible for copyright.

Say, for instance, that I have a brilliant idea for a movie: it's about an IP attorney who helps e-sellers during the day and secretly fights crime at night. I can't copyright that idea, but I could sit down and write the script and then copyright that manuscript. Copyrights can also be granted for recordings, whether they are of the Boston Philharmonic or a voice memo you dictated in a grocery store parking lot. But again, what's crucial is that you can only protect your manifestation of the idea, not the idea itself.

That's a good thing. We want a culture in which people have freedom of expression and the opportunity to offer their own creative interpretation. Undoubtedly, the script I write for the heroic crime-fighting IP attorney will be different from the one Steven Spielberg writes, which in turn will be different from the one Wes Anderson creates. This desire to

1) **Pictorial, graphic, and sculptural works**.
   Materials under this category can include sketches,
   drawings, cartoons, paintings, photographs,
   slides, greeting cards, maps, charts, globes, jewelry,
   glassware, models, tapestries, fabric designs, and
   wallpapers.

2) **Literary works**. This includes novels, nonfiction
   manuscripts, poems, articles, essays, directories,
   advertisements, catalogues, speeches, e-books,
   blog articles, and computer programs.

2) **Sound recordings**. Works under this category
   include recorded instrumentation, voice, or
   sound effects (which can also include thunder,
   animal noises, and other sounds of nature if they
   are copyrighted by the persons who recorded
   them).

One of my clients specializes in curtains made out of textiles
printed with unique designs. Their company features a dozen
or so different designs, so a logical question they had for me
was whether or not they should seek a copyright for each one.
Often, my advice to clients such as this one is to protect each
and every one of their designs or images, especially if their

product is profitable and they expect that it will continue to be so for the next year.

One convenient way to protect images associated with a product is to group them together as a single collection. If, for instance, you are selling a cell phone charger on Amazon, you might have a dozen or even more images of the charger, each focusing on a different feature. All of those images can easily be grouped as a collection, so it could be protected under one copyright application, provided that the following conditions have been met:

- All the works in the group must be photographs.
- All the photographs must be *unpublished*.
- The group must include no more than 750 photographs.
- All the photographs must be created by the same author.
- The copyright claimant for each photograph must be the same person or organization.
- The applicant must provide a title for the group.
- The applicant must provide a sequentially numbered list containing a title and file name for each photograph in the group.

While most of these conditions are fairly straightforward, the definition of "unpublished" has remained unclear—even for IP attorneys. One strategy to avoid that confusion is to include "All Rights Reserved" or a copyright symbol © on an image; doing so establishes your intentions that viewers may share links to your content but may not copy your images to their website (which would be considered "publishing").

Of course, as an e-seller, you will have to make your own determinations about how much time, money, and effort are worth a copyright, particularly if it's for a product that isn't very profitable. And, unlike trademarks (which must be actively used in commerce to be valid), copyrights protect intellectual property regardless of how—or even if—it's ever publicly used. In other words, I could write a movie script and never show it to another human outside the Copyright Office and still enjoy all the benefits a certification can provide.

Registering Your Work

Applying for a copyright registration may be done either through the mail or online. Regardless which mode you select, you will need some basic information about the item or items you wish to copyright. This includes the work's title, date of completion and, if applicable, when it was first published. Say, for instance, that you just created a new line of novelty kitchenware called Krazy Kitchen and are marketing pot holders with irreverent phrases or images on them. You took a series of stylized, funny images of the pot holders and now want to make sure that those photographs are protected. When applying for a copyright, it may not be abundantly clear what the title of these images would be, so it's fine to call them something like "Product Photos of Krazy Kitchen Pot holders." The date of completion would be when you took the photographs, and you would be considered both the author and copyright claimant (a fancy way of saying the person or organization applying for the copyright). Things get a little trickier if you hired someone to take the photographs: depending upon the nature of your agreement with that photographer, that person may be considered the author or even the claimant. If you are using a vendor to create your images, it's always a good idea to consult with an IP attorney to ensure you are protected and have the appropriate contracts or releases in place.

All copyright applications must also include a *mandatory deposit*. Simply put, a mandatory deposit is two complete copies of whatever work you seek to protect. The US Copyright Office has very specific rules about when and if this work should be submitted as electronic or hard copies. If the work you want to submit is either unpublished or was first published online, it will probably be required in an electronic format; however, you or your attorney will want to be sure to consult the full submission guidelines to be sure.

Once you have submitted your full copyright application, you can expect to wait anywhere from forty-five days to four or five months, depending upon the complexity of your application, the number of applications ahead of you in the queue, and whether or not your application was complete and correct. On average, applications submitted online are processed about twice as quickly as those submitted through the mail, which is definitely a good reason to opt for the former.

Once your application has been approved, you will be issued a copyright certificate of registry such as the following:

Certificate of Registration

This Certificate issued under the seal of the Copyright
Office in accordance with title 17, *United States Code*,
attests that registration has been made for the work
identified below. The information on this certificate has
been made a part of the Copyright Office records.

Marie Strong

Acting United States Register of Copyrights and Director

Registration Number
TX 8-835-791
Effective Date of Registration:
November 19, 2019
Registration Decision Date:
February 12, 2020

Title

Title of Work: Do I Need a Trademark? Everything You Should Know About Trademarks

Completion/Publication

Year of Completion: 2019
Date of 1st Publication: November 16, 2019
Nation of 1ˢᵗ Publication: United States

Author

- **Author:** ESQgo, PC
  Author Created: text
  Work made for hire: Yes
  Citizen of: United States

Copyright Claimant

Copyright Claimant: ESQgo, PC
303 North Glenoaks Boulevard Suite 200, Burbank, CA, 91502, United States

Limitation of copyright claim

Material excluded from this claim: photograph(s)

New material included in claim: text

Rights and Permissions

Organization Name: ESQgo, PC
Address: 303 North Glenoaks Boulevard Suite 200
Burbank, CA 91502 United States

Certification

Page 1 of 2

Regardless of what choices you make in your application process, it's always advisable to consult with a qualified intellectual property attorney who can guide you in your decision-making. And, as with trademarks, what's most crucial about the application process is that you get it right the first time around. The key to a successful application often lies in the legal strategy and reasoning used to make your case for protection. A good IP attorney will ensure you make the strongest possible case: a critical component of any winning application. Not only can that lawyer help you determine if copyright is your best form of IP protection, but that individual can also discover any possible obstacles to your application before filing and can determine if you should seek additional IP protection for your material, including trademarks or patents.

Copyright Infringement and When to Take Legal Action

When discussing trademarks in Chapter 2, I introduced the term *confusingly similar*—that subjective distinction used to determine if a new trademark too closely resembles an existing one. A similar concept exists in the world of copyrights, and that's whether or not a new work is considered *substantially similar* to an existing one. When it comes to copyright law, it doesn't matter if the two companies attempting to use the copyright are distinct (as was the case with Delta Airlines and Delta Faucets). Works registered with a copyright are protected regardless of how they are used. In other words, it doesn't matter if you sell soap and I sell computers: if our artwork is substantially similar and copyrighted, one of us may well be in legal trouble.

Other examples of activities that would constitute copyright infringement if you carry them out without first obtaining permission from the owner, creator, or holder of the copyrighted material include:

- Recording a film in a movie theater
- Posting a video on your company's website that features copyrighted words or songs
- Using copyrighted images on your Amazon's product page
- Using a musical group's copyrighted songs on your company's website
- Modifying a copyrighted image to display your

product and then displaying it on your company's website or on Amazon

- Creating merchandise for sale that features copyrighted words or images
- Downloading music or films without paying for their use
- Copying any literary or artistic work without a license or written agreement

The best way to avoid copyright infringement is to not use any work that you yourself did not create. That includes materials found on the internet, which are almost never fair game.

To establish direct copyright infringement, a plaintiff must demonstrate ownership of a valid copyright, and that another party has illegally reproduced the copyrighted work. Most often, that is demonstrated because a plaintiff can prove substantial similarities between their copyrighted work and a defendant's reproduction.

What constitutes "substantially" similar when it comes to copyright? As with trademarks, it can be difficult to say. Some IP experts attempt to assign a percentage to the question; they'll say, for instance, that a design is safe to use if you've changed at least 30 percent of it. I find that reasoning more than suspect. Assigning a quantitative number when comparing an original and duplicate work can easily become a fool's errand. And there is no statute guaranteeing that you are in the clear even if you can prove you've only borrowed 70 percent of a work—plus, how would you even quantify a percentage to the similarities?

In the world of intellectual property law, the Ninth Circuit Court of Appeals is considered one of the most influential when it comes to copyright matters, since it has jurisdiction over California, widely considered the geographic hub not just for film and TV, but also music, software, and gaming. The Ninth Circuit uses two different tests to determine substantial similarity. The first is an "extrinsic" test in which all unprotectable aspects of a plaintiff's work are first removed and then the remaining elements of the work are compared to the defendant's in order to objectively assess the similarities. The second test is "intrinsic" and takes a holistic, subjective approach to determine whether an ordinary person would consider the two works as substantially similar.

For a plaintiff to establish a substantial similarity in the Ninth Circuit, they must succeed under both the intrinsic and extrinsic tests. For that reason, I tend to advise my clients based on their appetite for conflict. If they have the resources to withstand a legal challenge, I might be more inclined to go after a competitor or encourage them to try their hand at pushing up against an existing copyright. That said, it's always important to begin by considering what resources are also available to the other party. As Sun Tzu once said, "Every battle is won before it's ever fought." Knowing what legal resources your opposition has available to them, as well as their history of litigation, can tell you a lot about what you will be up against, should you choose to proceed with legal action. For instance, if your opposition is resource-poor and has no history of litigation, beginning with a "cease and desist" letter may be enough to resolve the copyright infringement. A qualified IP attorney will help you make this kind of assessment and weigh the merits of your case. But always keep in mind: we aren't fortune tellers. I've seen plenty of cases that appeared cut and dried, only to become a war of attrition and resources. In other words, just because the merits are in your favor does not mean you will be victorious.

A particularly difficult situation many of my clients find themselves in is believing they own the rights to some of the materials they post on their seller sites, particularly when those materials are photographs or other images. Many sellers obtain images believing that they then become the owners of those images, but that isn't always the case. Copyright law in the United States is structured such that the person who made an image, even if it's a photograph, retains ownership of that image. The same is true for copywriters who prepare commercial content. Too often, new clients have come to me, confused and frustrated, because images of their products have been flagged or even removed from their seller sites. In the end, it almost always turns out that that is because they don't actually retain ownership—instead, that belongs to the photographer who shot the image.

To avoid this costly hassle, always use a *work for hire* agreement when contracting out any work that might be eligible for a copyright. This simple document protects both an independent contractor and the company or person hiring them; it also ensures that you obtain and retain rights to any work completed under that contract. Doing so doesn't just protect you from a potentially unscrupulous contractor: it also helps during a dispute with a competitor. How? Imagine that you have spent a substantial sum on professional photographs depicting your new line of bath mats. One of your competitors sells a similar product and so decides to copy and paste your photographs to their own page, simply photoshopping their logo wherever yours once appeared. Were you to seek legal action against your competitor, one of the first questions asked by an IP attorney or the courts would be who maintains ownership of the images. Without that work for hire contract, you will have no way of proving that you are the rightful owner—since you will not be able to procure a copyright registration without a work for hire agreement. As a result, you may not be able to seek compensation or even demand that your competitor cease using the images. A helpful analogy is that of buying a used car: you may physically possess the car but without a bill of sale, you have no way of proving you own the vehicle. And that can make it difficult if not impossible to seek damages if you are rear-ended by another driver.

Unlike trademarks, there is no online database to search to determine whether prior copyrights exist. There are websites that can be searched for particular genres, such as electronic music, but even finding a title or reprint of lyrics still means that an IP attorney—and possibly a judge—will have to interpret just how similar the two works really are. Another option is hiring a service provider in Washington, DC, who can visit the Library of Congress and search on your behalf, but the cost of doing so can be prohibitive for many small-scale e-sellers, especially if they need to consult multiple files there. Therefore, here are some general tips on avoiding copyright infringement:

1) Have a general idea of what copyright laws protect.
2) If you did not create the work or it was not a "work made for hire" then don't use it.
3) The works you find on the internet should generally not be used.

It's also important to note that there are special protections in place for internet content providers and members of the digital marketplace. In 1998, Congress passed the Digital Millennium Copyright Act (DMCA), which updated copyright law in three important ways. First, it extended protections for copyright owners using digital formats, particularly those that are password protected. It also made it a crime to provide false copyright information or to unfairly alter existing copyright information. Finally, it afforded additional protections and powers to online service providers, including Amazon, eBay, and even commercial sites like Barnes & Noble. This last category has had sweeping impacts on the digital marketplace. Perhaps most notably, it shields online service providers like Amazon from copyright infringement liability. In other words, if a competitor steals your copyrighted materials and uses them as their own, you may not sue Amazon for any damages. But what the DMCA also does is enables those same providers to remove infringing content without the need for litigation or other legal proceedings.

This has been a real boon for Amazon users. Today, any seller can approach Amazon with notice that another seller is infringing on their copyright. Amazon will then take down the infringing material and notify that seller. There are also mechanisms in place if you feel that you have been wrongly accused of copyright infringement at an online service provider's site. The DMCA allows for a counternotice, or a statement attesting that you have not, in fact, infringed on an existing copyright and requesting that your content be restored to your page. At that point, the other party has ten business days to file a lawsuit. If they fail to do so, the content may be restored by the marketplace.

As I mentioned in the introduction to this book, Amazon is in many ways its own sovereign nation, complete with its own laws and legal processes. Just as Amazon often requires a registered or pending trademark in order to pursue its trademark complaint system (and recall that US courts *do not* require this), so too does the e-commerce giant invert the copyright litigation process. Namely, a seller is not required to provide any proof of copyright registration in order to pursue a copyright complaint at Amazon, whereas a copyright registration is required to file a copyright infringement lawsuit in federal court.

That said, if you want to protect your e-commerce brand and the original work associated with it, you'll want to strongly consider a formal copyright application. Copyrights may not have the teeth of a trademark, but they are an important part of the intellectual property process and can go a long way toward ensuring that your original work is not stolen or used without your permission.

CHAPTER 4

Patents

IN 1995, MONSANTO MADE INTERNATIONAL NEWS WHEN THE company announced it had received patent approval for a genetically engineered potato capable of fighting insect predation without the addition of pesticides. The potato, known as "New Leaf," had been bioengineered to produce its own insecticide: a bacterial toxin deadly only to beetles and other pests. The idea of a genetically modified potato— and the process used to create it—were highly controversial at the time. Environmentalists saw it as evidence of a franken-food Armageddon; commercial potato growers saw it as a welcome end to years of spraying costly and dangerous chemicals.

But the scientific advances that made this patent possible continued, and by the turn of this century, American farms contained over fifty million acres of GMO crops, as did farms in countries as far flung as India and Brazil. What distinguished these crops wasn't just the biotechnology behind them; it was also the fact that—for one of the first times in history—the seed used to grow them was considered intellectual property.

For centuries, farmers have preserved seeds from one year's harvest in order to plant the next (a process they commonly call "saving seeds"). Monsanto put an end to that practice for many by requiring its growers to sign complicated contracts stipulating that they would not save any of their patented seeds, nor would they grow them close enough to other crops that the plants would be able to cross-pollinate. Breaking that contract was considered patent infringement and could result in hundreds of thousands of dollars in legal damages.

The constitutionality of that contract was put to a test in 2013, when Monsanto brought a case against an Indiana farmer to the United States Supreme Court, alleging that he had violated Monsanto's intellectual property rights when he bought generic seeds containing the protein Monsanto had created for its genetically modified products. The Supreme Court backed Monsanto unanimously, in what many legal scholars saw as a bellwether test of patent sovereignty in this country. Similar cases in Brazil and Canada were also found in favor of Monsanto, again affirming that farmers do not really own the seeds they purchase from Monsanto and that they cannot save and plant them in subsequent years.

Today, the seed giant has over seven thousand patents worldwide, each covering a similar innovation or technology. Every one of those patents underwent a lengthy application and review process to ensure that Monsanto's intellectual property has the maximum protections available. And while you may see your presence in the digital marketplace as worlds away from this Fortune 500 seed behemoth, you too may benefit from the robust protections provided by a patent.

Some of the most common questions I receive from Amazon sellers relate to patents. Clients want to know if sourcing products overseas might be an infringement of an existing patent. They also often ask how they can create and protect their own unique product so that they can differentiate themselves from their competitors (and prevent those competitors from capitalizing on their innovations). They also want help distinguishing when it's best to apply for a trademark or trade dress versus a patent.

When it comes to protecting intellectual property, patents are both far more complicated and expensive than copyrights and trademarks. But dollar for dollar, they are also your best protection—especially in the long run. (Utility patents usually last twenty years from the date of filing; design patents are good for fifteen years from the date of grant.) In this chapter, we'll explore the different types of patents available, the patent application process, and what constitutes patent infringement.

Types of Patents

The USPTO defines a patent as the grant of a property right to an inventor for their innovation. More specifically, a patent offers its holder "the right to exclude others from making, using, offering for sale, or selling" any innovation protected by the patent. While a trademark can protect your brand, a patent can protect the exclusive rights of the particular innovations or products sold by that brand. Patents can be obtained for inventions, such as a jet propulsion pack or even a new twist on a garlic press. They can be obtained for novel composites (say, a more durable concrete for house siding). They can protect the ornamental design or appearance of a new computer keyboard. They can also protect the processes that create these innovations (Henry Ford's assembly line is a particularly noteworthy example).

Here in the United States, there are three different types of patents. The first is for a *utility patent*, or a patent that protects a new machine, article, or process. Say, for instance, that I invented a new four-sided writing instrument that has roller-tip ink pens on two ends, along with highlighters on the other two sides. The actual writing instrument could be eligible for a utility patent. If the way I manufacture these pens is also new and novel, I could receive a second utility patent for that as well.

Design patents, on the other hand, protect the ornamental design or appearance of an article but not the functionality. Put another way, a utility patent protects a particular innovation, both in terms of how it works and how it's built, whereas a design patent protects how that innovation looks. Using my four-sided pen example, then, I could also apply for a design patent protecting the unique appearance of my writing instrument.

The final type of patent is a *plant patent*, which (as its name suggests) protects new varieties of plants. That type, of course, wouldn't help me and my new writing implement, but it has made Monsanto the $21 billion company it is today.

For an innovation to be protected by a patent, it must be considered "useful," which is to say that it must perform its intended function (a garlic press that doesn't actually press garlic cloves, for instance, wouldn't be eligible). An idea of a solar-powered flying hoverboard probably also wouldn't be eligible, unless you can prove to the USPTO that it actually works (and if you can, by all means give me a call: I'd love to be your first customer).

A patent must also protect a human invention, rather than something that occurs in nature (which is why Monsanto couldn't patent a naturally occurring potato, but it can protect one that it has genetically engineered). And unlike a trademark, which can only protect something actively being used in commerce, you can patent a new innovation, even if you never intend to manufacture, sell, or use it.

The Patent Application Process

The first requirement for a patent of any sort is that the invention you wish to protect must both be capable of being used and provide a clear benefit. In the case of my hypothetical writing instrument, I might have one of the pens write in red and the other in black, which could provide a clear benefit for teachers marking papers.

The second requirement is that the invention must be new or novel. As with trademarks, you will want to conduct a thorough search of existing patents before making your application. This can be done by any applicant; however, I always recommend hiring a qualified IP attorney. A simple search of "pen" on the USPTO patent database, for instance, yields thousands of categories ranging from foldable playpens for toddlers, feed pens for cattle, fountain pens, ball-pens used in physical therapy, and many, many more. A good IP attorney can successfully navigate these categories to ensure that your search is as accurate as it is thorough.

It's very rare for a patent search to come back with no matches. Most often, an IP attorney will find a spectrum of patents that may have some elements similar to your innovation. Your legal counsel should be able to tell you whether or not it's worth proceeding and what risks, if any, might be associated with that decision. If you decide to go forward, your next step will be to actually begin your patent application. Here again, hiring an IP attorney can go a long way towards ensuring that your application is complete and that it is approved. The USPTO receives approximately five hundred thousand patent applications a year. Each is routed to a particular technology center within the USPTO which is staffed by examiners who have expertise in that area, whether it's biotechnology and agriculture, computer networks, transportation, or another.

As with trademark applications, a successful patent application will be as broad as possible to minimize ways your competition can encroach on your idea. For instance, I might choose to describe my four-sided writing implement as a "two-way pen and two-way highlighter." Doing so grants me a lot more protection than if I were to describe it as "a four-sided pen with black ink on one side, red ink on the other, and two highlighters at the other ends." In that case, there would be little preventing my competition from patenting another writing implement featuring blue and red ink, or another variation on that theme. A skilled IP attorney knows that every single word matters on a patent application and how to use those words to your best advantage.

Patents are technical documents, so they also include extensive descriptions and illustrations. One of my favorite examples is a utility patent for a UFO, which the US Navy received in 2018. I've included a copy of the patent certificate below.

US010144532B2

(12) **United States Patent**
Pais

(10) Patent No.: US 10,144,532 B2
(45) Date of Patent: Dec. 4, 2018

(54) **CRAFT USING AN INERTIAL MASS REDUCTION DEVICE**

(71) Applicant: **Salvatore Cezar Pais**, Leonardtown, MD (US)

(72) Inventor: **Salvatore Cezar Pais**, Leonardtown, MD (US)

(73) Assignee: **The United States of America as represented by the Secretary of the Navy**, Washington, DC (US)

(*) Notice: Subject to any disclaimer, the term of this patent is extended or adjusted under 35 U.S.C. 154(b) by 153 days.

(21) Appl. No.: **15/141,270**

(22) Filed: **Apr. 28, 2016**

(65) **Prior Publication Data**

US 2017/0313446 A1   Nov. 2, 2017

(51) **Int. Cl.**
B64G 1/40   (2006.01)

(52) **U.S. Cl.**
CPC *B64G 1/409* (2013.01)

(58) **Field of Classification Search**
CPC B64G 1/409
See application file for complete search history.

(56) **References Cited**

PUBLICATIONS

Froning, H. David, Quantum Vacuum Engineering for Power and Propulsion from the Energetics of Space, Third International Con-

ference on Future Energy, Oct. 9-10, 2009, Washington, DC, US.
Pais, Salvatore, Conditional Possibility of Spacecraft Propulsion at Superluminal Speeds, Intl. J. Space Science and Engineering, 2015, vol. 3, No. 1, Inderscience Enterprises Ltd.
Puthoff, H.E., Polarizable-Vacuum (PV) Approach to General Relativity, Foundations of Physics, Jun. 2002, vol. 32, No. 6.
Prigogine, Ilya, Time, Structure and Fluctuations, Nobel Lecture, Dec. 8, 1977, Brussels, Belgium and Austin, Texas.
Hayasaka, Hideo and Takeuchi, Sakae, Anomalous Weight Reduction on a Gyroscope's Right Rotations around the Vertical Axis on the Earth, The American Physical Society, Physical Review Letters, Dec. 18, 1989, vol. 63, No. 25, Japan.
Pais, Salvatore, The High Energy Electromagnetic Field Generator, Int. J. Space Science and Engineering, 2015, vol. 3, No. 4, Inderscience Enterprises, Ltd.

Primary Examiner — Philip J Bonzell

(74) *Attorney, Agent, or Firm* — Mark O Glut; NAWCAD

(57)   **ABSTRACT**

A craft using an inertial mass reduction device comprises of an inner resonant cavity wall, an outer resonant cavity, and microwave emitters. The electrically charged outer resonant cavity wall and the electrically insulated inner resonant cavity wall form a resonant cavity. The microwave emitters create high frequency electromagnetic waves throughout the resonant cavity causing the resonant cavity to vibrate in an accelerated mode and create a local polarized vacuum outside the outer resonant cavity wall.

4 Claims, 1 Drawing Sheet

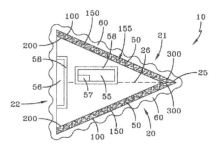

U.S. Patent   Dec. 4, 2018   US 10,144,532 B2

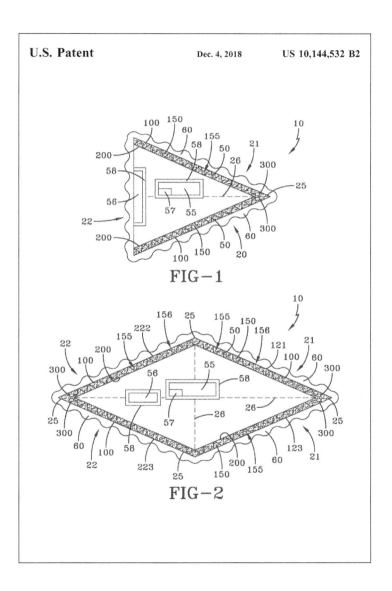

FIG—1

FIG—2

US 10,144,532 B2

1

CRAFT USING AN INERTIAL MASS REDUCTION DEVICE

STATEMENT OF GOVERNMENT INTEREST

The invention described herein may be manufactured and used by or for the Government of the United States of America for governmental purposes without payment of any royalties thereon or therefor.

BACKGROUND

There are four known fundamental forces which control matter and, therefore, control energy. The four known forces are strong nuclear forces, weak nuclear forces, electromagnetic force, and gravitational force. In this hierarchy of forces, the electromagnetic force is perfectly positioned to be able to manipulate the other three. A stationary electric charge gives rise to an electric (electrostatic) field, while a moving charge generates both an electric and a magnetic field (hence the electromagnetic field). Additionally, an accelerating charge induces electromagnetic radiation in the form of transverse waves, namely light. Mathematically, as well as physically, electromagnetic field intensity can be represented as the product of electric field strength and magnetic field strength. Electromagnetic fields act as carriers for both energy and momentum, thus interacting with physical entities at the most fundamental level.

Artificially generated high energy electromagnetic fields, such as those generated with a high energy electromagnetic field generator (HEEMFG), interact strongly with the vacuum energy state. The vacuum energy state can be described as an aggregate/collective state, comprised of the superposition of all quantum fields' fluctuations permeating the entire fabric of spacetime. High energy interaction with the vacuum energy state can give rise to emergent phenomena, such as force and matter fields' unification. According to quantum field theory, this strong interaction between the fields is based on the mechanism of transfer of vibrational energy between the fields. The transfer of vibrational energy further induces local fluctuations in adjacent quantum fields which permeate spacetime (these fields may or may not be electromagnetic in nature). Matter, energy, and spacetime are all emergent constructs which arise out of the fundamental framework that is the vacuum energy state.

Everything that surrounds us, ourselves included, can be described as macroscopic collections of fluctuations, vibrations, and oscillations in quantum mechanical fields. Matter is confined energy, bound within fields, frozen in a quantum of time. Therefore, under certain conditions (such as the coupling of hyper-frequency axial spin with hyper-frequency vibrations of electrically charged systems) the rules and special effects of quantum field behavior also apply to macroscopic physical entities (macroscopic quantum phenomena).

Moreover, the coupling of hyper-frequency gyrational (axial rotation) and hyper-frequency vibrational electrodynamics is conducive to a possible physical breakthrough in the utilization of the macroscopic quantum fluctuations vacuum plasma field (quantum vacuum plasma) as an energy source (or sink), which is an induced physical phenomenon.

The quantum vacuum plasma (QVP) is the electric glue of our plasma universe. The Casimir Effect, the Lamb Shift, and Spontaneous Emission, are specific confirmations of the existence of QVP.

2

It is important to note that in region(s) where the electromagnetic fields are strongest, the more potent the interactions with the QVP, therefore, the higher the induced energy density of the QVP particles which spring into existence (the Dirac Sea of electrons and positrons). These QVP particles may augment the obtained energy levels of the HEEMFG system, in that energy flux amplification may be induced.

It is possible to reduce the inertial mass and hence the gravitational mass, of a system/object in motion, by an abrupt perturbation of the non-linear background of local spacetime (the local vacuum energy state), equivalent to an accelerated excursion far from thermodynamic equilibrium (analogous with symmetry-breaking induced by abrupt changes of state/phase transitions). The physical mechanism which drives this diminution in inertial mass is based on the negative pressure (hence repulsive gravity) exhibited by the polarized local vacuum energy state (local vacuum polarization being achieved by a coupling of accelerated high frequency vibration with accelerated high frequency axial rotation of an electrically charged system/object) in the close proximity of the system/object in question. In other words, inertial mass reduction can be achieved via manipulation of quantum field fluctuations in the local vacuum energy state, in the immediate proximity of the object/system. Therefore it is possible to reduce a craft's inertia, that is, its resistance to motion/acceleration by polarizing the vacuum in the close proximity of the moving craft.

Polarization of the local vacuum is analogous to manipulation/modification of the local space tie topological lattice energy density. As a result, extreme speeds can be achieved.

If we can engineer the structure of the local quantum vacuum state, we can conscript the fabric of our reality at the most fundamental level (thus affecting a physical system's inertial and gravitational properties). This realization would greatly advance the fields of aerospace propulsion and power generation.

The physical equation which describes the maximum intensity achieved by the high energy electromagnetic field generator (HEEMFG) system is described by the magnitude of the Poynting vector, which in non-relativistic for (accounting for all three modes of motion) can be written as:

$$S_{max} = f_G(\sigma^2/\varepsilon_0) \ [R_s\omega + R_v v + v_R] \qquad \text{(Equation 1),}$$

where f_G is the HEEMFG system geometric shape factor (equal to 1 for a disc configuration), σ is the surface charge density (total electric charge divided by surface area of the HEEMFG system), ε_0 is the electrical permittivity of free space, R_s is the radius of rotation (disc radius), ω is the angular frequency of rotation in rad/s, R_v is the vibration (harmonic oscillation) amplitude, v is the angular frequency of vibration in Hertz, and the term v_R is the curvilinear translation speed (acquired via a propulsive unit of either chemical, nuclear or magneto-plasma-dynamic (VASIMR) type attached to the HEEMFG system—the integrated unit being the craft).

Therefore, if we consider only rotation, given a disc configuration, with σ=50,000 Coulombs/m², a disc (spinning/axially rotating) radius of 2 m and an angular speed of 30,000 RPM, an generate an electromagnetic (EM) field intensity (S_{max} is the rate of energy flow per unit area, or energy flux) value on the order of 10^{24} Watts/m² (this value does not account for any QVP interactions).

Furthermore, if we couple the high frequency of rotation with high vibration (harmonic oscillation) frequencies in the range of 10^9 to 10^{18} Hertz (and above) we can obtain S_{max} intensity values in the range 10^{24} to 10^{28} Watts/m² (and

3

beyond). These extremely high EM field intensity values emphasize the novelty of this concept, especially suited for the design of energy generation machinery with power output levels much higher than those currently achievable.

For the case of an accelerating angular frequency of vibration ($a_{max} = R_v v^2$), neglecting rotation and curvilinear translation, Equation 1 becomes (note intrinsic significance of acceleration):

$$S_{max} = f_q(\sigma^2/\epsilon_0) \left[(R_s x^2) \, t_{op} \right] \qquad \text{(Equation 2)}$$

where t_{op} is the operational time for which the charged electrical system s accelerating in its vibration.

Close inspection of Equation 2 results in an important realization, namely: strong local interaction with the high energetics of the quantum vacuum fields' fluctuations superposition (macroscopic vacuum energy state) is possible in a laboratory environment, by application of high frequency gyration (axial spin) and/or high frequency vibration of minimally charged objects (order of unity surface charge density), in an acceleration mode. In this manner, a high degree of local vacuum energy polarization can be achieved.

To illustrate this fact, considering a high end microwave frequency on the order of 10^{11} Hertz, a surface charge density on the order of 1 C/m^2 and an operational time on the order of the inverse of the vibrational amplitude, we obtain an energy flux value of 10^{33} W/m^2. This exceptionally high power intensity induces a pair production avalanche, thereby ensuring complete polarization of the local vacuum state.

Local polarization of the vacuum in the close proximity of a craft equipped with an HEEMFG system would have the effect of cohering the highly energetic and random quantum vacuum fields' fluctuations, which virtually block the path of an accelerating craft, in such a manner that the resulting negative pressure of the polarized vacuum allows less labored motion through it (as noted by H. David Froning).

Spontaneous electron-positron pair production out of the vacuum is a strong indicator of vacuum polarization being achieved. Julian Schwinger (Nobel prize winning physicist) gives a value of the electric field (E) on the order of 10^{18} V/m, for this phenomenon to take place. The mass production rate $(dm/dt)_{pp}$ of particle/anti-particle pairs can be expressed in terms of S_{max} (energy flux), namely:

$$2\gamma (dm/dt)_{pp} c^2 = S_{max} A_S \qquad \text{(Equation 3)}$$

where A_S is the surface area from which the energy flux emanates, c is the speed of light in free space, and γ is the relativistic stretch factor $[1-(v^2/c^2)]^{-1/2}$. Note that the pair production rate increases with increasing energy flux from the craft's generated electromagnetic field. Therefore, the level, to which the vacuum is polarized, thus allowing less labored motion through it, strictly depends on the artificially generated electromagnetic energy flux.

If we consider the boundary condition in the close proximity of the craft where the energy density of the artificially generated electromagnetic (EM) field equals the local energy density of the polarized vacuum (caused in part by the local zero-point vacuum fluctuations on the order of 10^{-15} Joules/cm^3 and in part by the artificial EM field interacting with the local vacuum energy state) we can write the approximate equivalence:

$$(S_{max}/c) = [(h^* v_v^4)/8\pi^2 c^3] \qquad \text{(Equation 4)}$$

where c is the speed of light in free space, (h^*) is Planck's constant divided by (2π) and (v_v) is the frequency of quantum fluctuations in the vacuum (modeled as harmonic oscillators). Furthermore, given that the left side of Equation 4 is on the order of $(\epsilon_0 E^2)$ where E is the artificially

4

generated electric field (strength), considering the Schwinger value of (E) for the onset of spontaneous pair production, we obtain a (v_v) value on the order of 10^{22} Hertz, which matches our expectations, since the Dirac virtual pair production, results in total annihilation, yielding gamma rays, which occupy the electromagnetic frequency spectrum of 10^{19} Hertz and above.

A recent paper, by the inventor, published in the International Journal of Space Science and Engineering (Pais, S. C., Vol. 3, No. 1, 2015) considers the conditional possibility of superluminal craft propulsion in a Special Relativity framework. It is observed that under certain physical conditions, the singularity expressed by the relativistic stretch factor 'gamma' as the craft's speed (v) approaches the speed of light (c). is no longer present in the physical picture. This involves the instantaneous removal of energy-mass from the system (craft) when the craft's speed reaches (v=c/2). The author discusses the possibility of using exotic matter (negative mass/negative energy density) to bring about this effect. This may not have to be the only alternative. The artificial generation of gravity waves in the locality of the craft, can result in energy-mass removal (gravity waves are propagating fluctuations in gravitational fields, whose amplitude and frequency are a function of the motion of the masses involved).

Moreover, it is feasible to remove energy-mass from the system by enabling vacuum polarization, as discussed by Harold Puthoff, in that diminution of inertial (and thus gravitational) mass can be achieved via modification of quantum field fluctuations in the vacuum. In other words, it is possible to reduce a craft's inertia, that is, its resistance to motion/acceleration by polarizing the vacuum in the close proximity of the moving craft. As a result, extreme speeds can be achieved.

Vacuum energy state can be thought of as a chaotic system comprised of random, highly energetic fluctuations in the collective quantum fields which define it. Considering Ilya Prigogine's Nobel Prize work on far from equilibrium thermodynamics (the Prigogine effect), a chaotic system can self-organize if subjected to three conditions, namely: the system must be non-linear, it must experience an abrupt excursion far from thermodynamic equilibrium, and it must be subjected to an energy flux (order from chaos).

An artificially generated high energy/high frequency electromagnetic field (such as the fields an HEEMFG can produce) can fulfill all three conditions simultaneously (especially in an accelerated vibration/rotation mode), when strongly interacting with the local vacuum energy state. These interactions are induced by the coupling of hyper-frequency axial rotation (spin) and hyper-frequency vibration (harmonic oscillations/abrupt pulsations) of electrically charged systems (high energy electromagnetic field generators), placed on the outside of the craft in strategic locations.

In this manner, local vacuum polarization, namely the coherence of vacuum fluctuations within the immediate proximity of the craft's surface (outside vacuum boundary) is achieved, allowing for 'smooth sailing' through the negative pressure (repulsive gravity) of the 'void' (the void within the vacuum). It may be stated that the void 'sucks in' the craft.

It is of extreme importance that the craft has the ability to control the accelerated modes of vibration and spin of the electrically charged surfaces, in particular the rapid rates of change of accelerated-decelerated-accelerated vibration and/or accelerated-decelerated-accelerated gyration (axial spin) of the electrified surfaces. In this manner we can delay the onset of relaxation to thermodynamic equilibrium, thus

US 10,144,532 B2

| 5 | 6 |

generating a physical mechanism which may induce anomalous effects (such as inertial or gravitational mass reduction). Furthermore, it is possible to enable the Gertsenshtein Effect, namely the production of high frequency gravitational waves by high frequency electromagnetic radiation, in this manner modifying the gravitational fields in close proximity to the craft, resulting in its propulsion.

For the mathematical formalism of inertial (and thus gravitational) mass reduction consider that in a published Physical Review Letter (December 1989), Hayasaka and Takeuchi report the anomalous weight reduction of gyroscopes for right rotations only. At the time, the authors could not elucidate the physics behind these anomalous results. Several null result experiments followed (a recent one as well) which declared the Hayasaka et al. results null and void, or at least questionable—however all these experiments were flawed in their ability to entirely duplicate the Hayasaka et al. experimental procedure and set-up (especially the high vacuum chamber the test section was mounted inside).

Closer attention to the non-zero intercept of the Hayasaka et al. expression relating the gyro's weight diminution with respect to its mass, its angular rotational frequency and its effective rotor radius, yields the possibility of a local quantum vacuum effect, namely a negative pressure (repulsive gravity) condition being present. This is due to the non-zero intercept being of the same order of magnitude with the Fokker-Planck electron-proton thermal equilibration rate (f_{ep}), given an approximate Hydrogen atom number density of 40 atoms/m³, commensurate with the local quantum vacuum state.

Consider the Hayasaka et al. expression for gyro-weight reduction, written in SI units as:

$$\Delta W_R(\omega) = -2 \times 10^{-10} \, M \, r_{eq} \, \omega \, \text{kg m s}^{-2} \qquad \text{(Equation 5)},$$

where ΔW_R is the reduction in weight, M is the mass of the rotor (in kg), ω is the angular frequency of rotation (in rad/s), and r_{eq} is the equivalent gyro-radius (in m).

From this relationship we see that the units of the non-zero intercept (2×10^{-10}) are (1/s). This non-zero intercept is endemic of the physics of gyro-rotational acceleration, in particular, the physical mechanism of abrupt excursion far from thermodynamic equilibrium.

We can further hypothesize that if the gyro-rotor was to vibrate uniformly (instead of rotating), and its vibration (harmonic oscillation) was to accelerate in frequency (thus inducing a state of abrupt departure far from thermodynamic equilibrium), it is possible that the resulting physics would be similar to that describing the rotational acceleration, thus we may write (using a simple dimensional analysis):

$$\Delta W_R(v) = -f_{ep} \, M \, A_v \, v \, \text{kg m s}^{-2} \qquad \text{(Equation 6)},$$

where f_{ep} is the Fokker-Planck electron-proton thermal equilibration rate, A_v is the vibration amplitude and v is frequency of vibration (in 1/s).

SUMMARY

The present invention is directed to a craft using an inertial mass reduction device. The craft includes an inner resonant cavity wall, an outer resonant cavity, and microwave emitters. The outer resonant cavity wall and the inner resonant cavity wall form a resonant cavity. The microwave emitters create high frequency electromagnetic waves throughout the resonant cavity causing the outer resonant cavity wall to vibrate in an accelerated mode and create a local polarized vacuum outside the outer resonant cavity wall.

It is a feature of the present invention to provide a craft, using an inertial mass reduction device, that can travel at extreme speeds.

DRAWINGS

These and other features, aspects and advantages of the present invention will become better understood with reference to the following description and appended claims, and accompanying drawings wherein:

FIG. 1 is an embodiment of the craft using an inertial mass reduction device; and

FIG. 2 is another embodiment of the craft using an inertial mass reduction device.

DESCRIPTION

The preferred embodiments of the present invention are illustrated by way of example below and in FIGS. 1-2. As shown in FIG. 1, the craft 10 using an inertial mass reduction device comprises of an outer resonant cavity wall 100, an inner resonant cavity 200, and microwave emitters 300. The outer resonant cavity wall 100 and the inner resonant cavity wall 200 form a resonant cavity 150. The microwave emitters 300 create high frequency electromagnetic waves 50 throughout the resonant cavity 150 causing the outer resonant cavity wall 100 to vibrate in an accelerated mode and create a local polarized vacuum 60 outside the outer resonant cavity wall 100.

In the description of the present invention, the invention will be discussed in a space, sea, air, or terrestrial environment; however, this invention can be utilized for any type of application that requires use of an inertial mass reduction device or use of a craft.

In the preferred embodiment, the resonant cavity 150 is filled with a noble gas 155. The gas xenon may be used; however, any noble gas 155 or the equivalent can be utilized. The gas is used for the plasma phase transition aspect of symmetry-breaking for amplification of the Prigogine effect. In addition, the resonant cavity 150 may be an annular duct. As shown in FIG. 1, the resonant cavity 150 may also surround a crew compartment 55, a power plant system 56, a cargo bay 57, or any other type of compartment. The crew compartment 55, power plant system 56, cargo bay 57, and the like can be guarded in a Faraday-type cage 58, against all EM radiation effects.

The craft 10, particularly the outer resonant cavity wall 100, may be electrically charged. In addition, the inner resonant cavity wall 200 may be electrically insulated, in order for the inner resonant cavity wall 200 not to vibrate. The craft 10 includes a main body 20 with a leading portion 21 and a trailing portion 22. Additionally, the craft 10 may include a frustum 25 or cone on its leading portion 21 of its main body 20. In one of the embodiments, the frustum 25 is rotatable about its own axis 26 or has the ability to rotate.

The microwave emitter(s) 300 may be an electromagnetic field generator. The preferred electromagnetic generator is the one described in U.S. patent application Ser. No. 14/807,943, entitled "Electromagnetic Field Generator and Method to Generate an Electromagnetic Field," filed on Jul. 24, 2015. The application is herein incorporated by reference, and has the same inventor. However, the microwave emitters 300 may be any type of microwave emitter or radio frequency emitter that is practicable.

As shown in FIGS. 1 and 2, the craft 10 has a plurality of microwave emitters 300. The microwave emitters 300 are arranged within the resonant cavity 150, and may be anten-

7

8

nas (high radio frequency emitter sources) in the electromagnetic (EM) spectrum range of 300 Megahertz to 300 Gigahertz. The plurality of microwave emitters **300** are arranged within the resonant cavity **150** such that the required electrical charge is present through the resonant cavity **150** in order to cause the outer resonant cavity wall **100** to vibrate in an accelerated mode.

As described, in one of its embodiments, the craft **10** utilizes microwave-induced vibration within a resonant annular cavity (the resonant cavity **150**). The manner and effectiveness with which the microwave energy couples with the outer resonant cavity wall **100** is called the cavity Q-factor (the inner resonant cavity wall **200** is electrically insulated and does not vibrate). This parameter can be written as the (energy stored/energy lost) ratio and is in the range of 10^4 to 10^9 (and beyond), depending on whether ordinary metal (Aluminum or Copper at room temperature) or cryogenically cooled superconducting material (Yttrium Barium Copper Oxide or Niobium) is used for the outer resonant cavity wall **100** and outside mold line skin of the craft. One must realize that the high energy/high frequency electromagnetic field generator responsible for the inertial mass diminution effect would generate a repulsive EM energy field while in earth's atmosphere, thereby repelling air molecules in its path of ascent/flight. Consequently, once in orbital space, by local vacuum polarization (quantum field fluctuations' modification/coherence), a repulsive gravity effect (recall the negative pressure of the polarized vacuum) would permit swift movement of the craft **10** (which can be, but without limitation, a cone or lenticular triangle/delta wing configuration).

It is possible to envision a hybrid aerospace/undersea craft (HAUC), which due to the physical mechanisms enabled with the inertial mass reduction device, can function as a submersible craft capable of extreme underwater speeds (lack of water-skin friction) and enhanced stealth capabilities (non-linear scattering of RF and sonar signals). This hybrid craft would move with great ease through the air/space/water mediums, by being enclosed in a vacuum plasma bubble/sheath, due to the coupled effects of EM field-induced air/water particles repulsion and vacuum energy polarization.

As shown in FIG. **2**, in another embodiment of the invention, the trailing portion **22** of the craft **10** is a mirror age of the leading portion **21**. This includes all working components internal to the craft. As shown in FIG. **2**, the leading portion **21** includes a top leading edge portion **121** and a bottom leading edge portion **123**, while the trailing portion **22** includes top trailing edge portion **222** and a bottom trailing edge portion **223**. Both the trailing portions **22** and leading portions **21** include an outer resonant cavity wall **100** and an inner resonant cavity wall **200** forming a

resonant cavity **150**, such the resonant cavity **150** shrouds, envelopes, or encapsulates the craft **10**. The outer resonant cavity wall **100**, inner resonant cavity wall **200**, and resonant cavity **150** that completely surrounds the craft **10** can be referred to as a resonant cavity shroud **156**. The microwave emitters **300** create high frequency electromagnetic waves throughout the entire resonant cavity shroud **156** causing the outer resonant cavity wall **100** (or a portion of the outer resonant cavity wall **100**) to vibrate and create a local polarized vacuum **60** outside the outer resonant cavity wall **100**.

In operation, in the preferred embodiment, the craft **10** may be powered to move in different directions by causing different sections of the resonant cavity shroud **156** to vibrate. For instance, to move upwards the top portion **156** (top leading edge portion **121** and top trailing edge portion **222**) of the resonant cavity shroud **156** is vibrated, thereby, causing the polarized vacuum field **60** to move the craft upward.

When introducing elements of the present invention or the preferred embodiment(s) thereof, the articles "a," "an," "the," and "said" are intended to mean there are one or more of the elements. The terms "comprising," "including," and "having" are intended to be inclusive and mean that there may be additional elements other than the listed elements.

Although the present invention has been described in considerable detail with reference to certain preferred embodiments thereof, other embodiments are possible. Therefore, the spirit and scope of the appended claims should not be limited to the description of the preferred embodiment(s) contained herein.

What is claimed is:

1. A craft using an inertial mass reduction device comprising:

an inner resonant cavity wall;

an outer resonant cavity wall, the inner resonant cavity wall and the outer resonant cavity wall forming a resonant cavity; and,

microwave emitters such that the microwave emitters create high frequency electromagnetic waves throughout the resonant cavity causing the outer resonant cavity wall to vibrate in an accelerated mode and create a local polarized vacuum outside the outer resonant cavity wall.

2. The craft of claim 1, wherein the resonant cavity is filled with a noble gas.

3. The craft of claim 1, wherein the outer resonant cavity wall is electrically charged.

4. The craft of claim 1, wherein the resonant cavity is axially rotated in an accelerated mode.

* * * * *

As you can see, the patent begins with basic information regarding the applicant and an overview of the object to be patented, followed by a more thorough description of what, in this case, is labeled a "craft using an inertial mass reduction device." Compare that to a design patent, such as this one for a card game table:

US00D633953S

(12) **United States Design Patent** (10) **Patent No.:** **US D633,953 S**

Katz (45) **Date of Patent:** ** **Mar. 8, 2011**

(54) **CARD GAME TABLE**

(76) Inventor: **Marcus A. Katz**, Miami Beach, FL (US)

(**) Term: **14 Years**

(21) Appl. No.: **29/364,164**

(22) Filed: **Jun. 18, 2010**

Related U.S. Application Data

(60) Division of application No. 29/339,635, filed on Jul. 2, 2009, now Pat. No. Des. 627,006, which is a continuation of application No. 12/348,150, filed on May 1, 2009, which is a continuation of application No. 12/090,851, filed on Apr. 18, 2008.

(51) LOC (9) Cl. **21-03**

(52) U.S. Cl. **D21/369**; D21/397

(58) **Field of Classification Search** D6/511;
D21/369, 385, 396–397; 273/274, 292; 463/13,
463/17, 20, 25, 46–47
See application file for complete search history.

(56) **References Cited**

U.S. PATENT DOCUMENTS

D161,845	S	*	2/1951	Larson	D21/397
D227,967	S	*	7/1973	Scarne	D21/397
D263,975	S	*	4/1982	Quiroga et al.	D21/369
5,275,416	A	*	1/1994	Schorr et al.	273/292
D345,767	S	*	4/1994	Ollington	D21/369
D361,350	S	*	8/1995	Nelson	D21/369
D365,853	S	*	1/1996	Zadro	D21/369
5,489,101	A	*	2/1996	Moody	273/292
5,782,472	A	*	7/1998	Brown	273/274
D397,732	S	*	9/1998	Serowik et al.	D21/369
5,921,550	A	*	7/1999	Awada	273/292
D421,466	S	*	3/2000	McBride	D21/369
D427,644	S	*	7/2000	Stern	D21/397
D452,283	S	*	12/2001	Regan et al.	D21/369
D467,624	S	*	12/2002	Boyd	D21/397
6,629,889	B2	*	10/2003	Mothwurf	463/25
D514,171	S	*	1/2006	Danellus	D21/397
D518,112	S	*	3/2006	Abbott et al.	D21/397
D521,569	S	*	5/2006	Rowe et al.	D21/397
D537,126	S	*	2/2007	Boyd et al.	D21/369
D548,799	S	*	8/2007	Looney et al.	D21/369
7,341,510	B2	*	3/2008	Bourbour et al.	463/13
D573,199	S	*	7/2008	Richani	D21/369
D578,575	S	*	10/2008	Clark et al.	D21/369
D579,056	S	*	10/2008	Murphy et al.	D21/369

* cited by examiner

Primary Examiner — Sandra Morris

(57) **CLAIM**

The ornamental design for a card game table, substantially as shown and described.

DESCRIPTION

FIG. 1 is a top plan view of the card game table, showing my new design;

FIG. 2 is a top plan view of a second embodiment thereof;

FIG. 3 is a top perspective view of a third embodiment thereof;

FIG. 4 is a top plan view thereof;

FIG. 5 is a top perspective view of a fourth embodiment thereof;

FIG. 6 is a top plan view thereof;

FIG. 7 is a cross-sectional view taken along line 7 — 7 in FIG. 2; and,

FIG. 8 is a cross-sectional view taken along line 8 — 8 in FIG. 2.

The broken line showing is for illustrative purposes only, and forms no part of the claimed design.

1 Claim, 7 Drawing Sheets

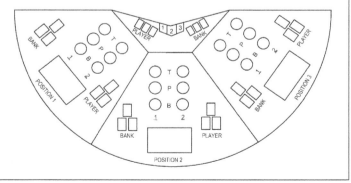

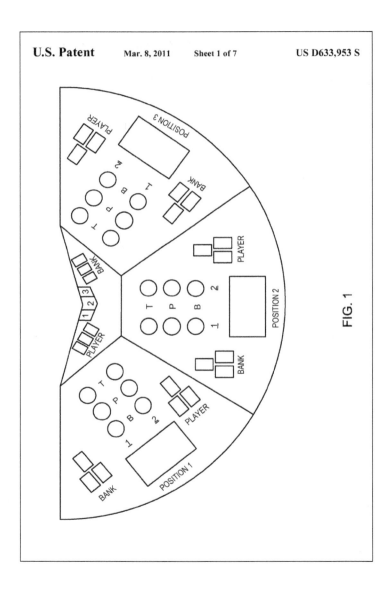

FIG. 1

U.S. Patent   Mar. 8, 2011   Sheet 2 of 7   US D633,953 S

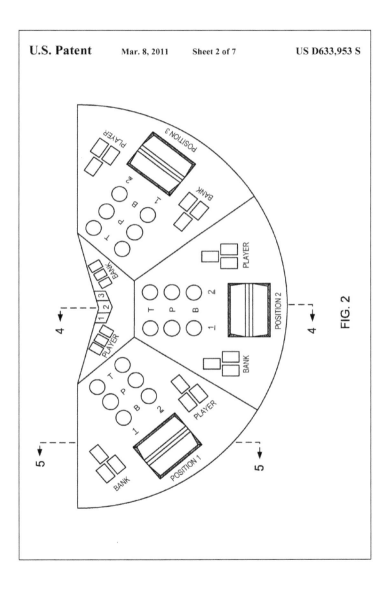

FIG. 2

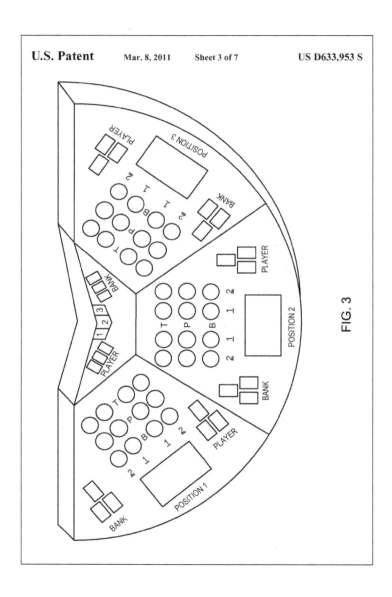

FIG. 3

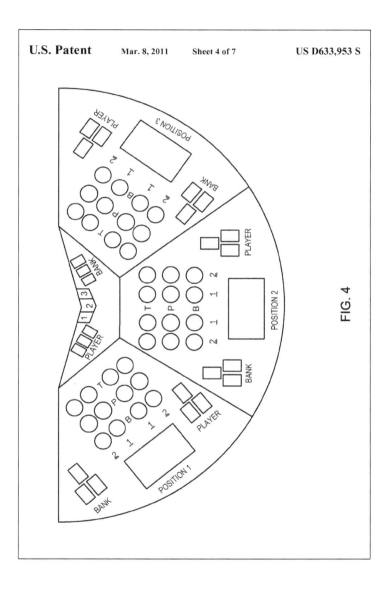

FIG. 4

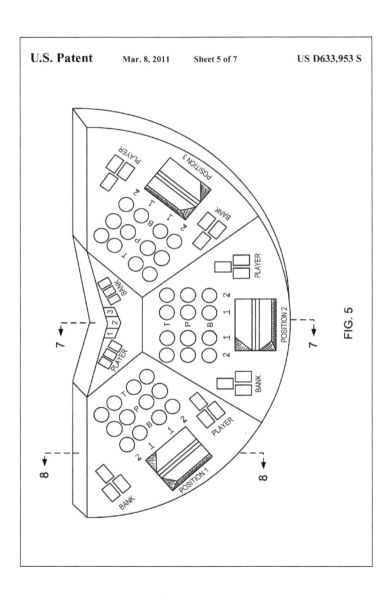

FIG. 5

U.S. Patent   Mar. 8, 2011   Sheet 6 of 7   US D633,953 S

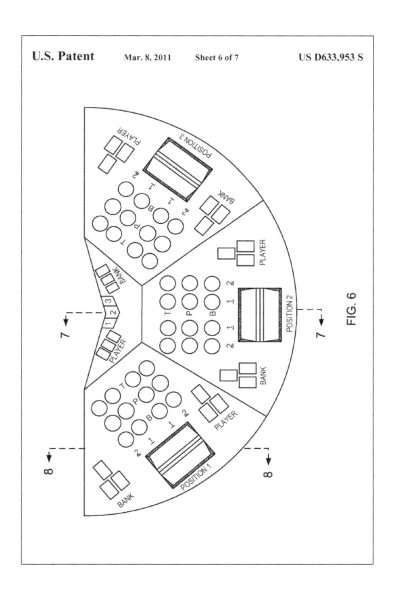

FIG. 6

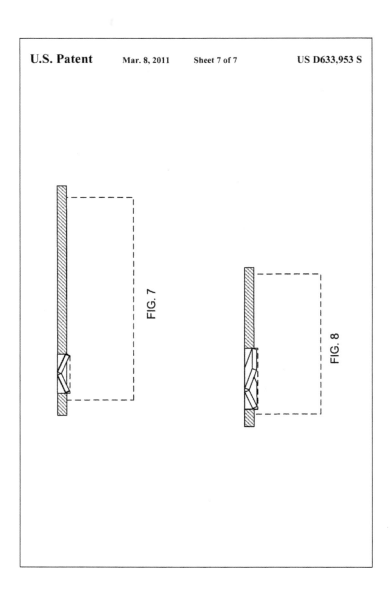

FIG. 7

FIG. 8

While the speculative UFO is undoubtedly a more sophisticated invention (or would be, were it to ever be built), the design patent for the card table is far more involved in terms of diagrams: evidence of the difference between the design patent, which protects the way an object looks and how it is built, versus a utility patent, which might best be considered as protecting the idea of the particular object.

Because a patent application is so involved, it's not uncommon for a design patent to take eighteen to twenty-four months from start to finish. A utility patent can take three times as long. It's not uncommon for the USPTO to reject or flag a patent application because of similar innovations already protected. This is another reason to retain a patent attorney, who can argue your case and the nuanced differences between what you are seeking to protect and what is already covered.

It's also worth noting that patent applications come with a hefty price tag that on average can range from $3,000–$15,000 for design patents and anywhere from $15,000 to several hundred thousand dollars for utility patents. That cost is just one more reason why it's always advisable to seek out a qualified IP attorney: they can help you determine if your innovation is worth the expenditures involved in the application process.

Patent Infringement

Just like with copyrights and trademarks, there is no guarantee that a successful patent application will prevent your competitors from infringing upon your intellectual property. Unfortunately, that means patent holders—particularly those selling in the digital marketplace—need to exhibit nearly constant vigilance.

Where patents are concerned, there are two primary types of infringement. The first is *literal infringement.* In this instance, a patent holder alleges that literally every aspect of their patent has been copied by the infringer. Most often, *literal infringement* is evoked when a competitor is either selling a plaintiff's actual products or attempting to market a copycat version. The good news for victims in these cases is that literal infringement is often very easy to prove, so the plaintiff's chance for success in court can be quite high.

The second type of patent infringement is known as *infringement under the doctrine of equivalents*. Simply put, this argument states that although a patented innovation and one infringing upon that patent may not be identical, they are either substantially similar or can be reasonably considered as substitutes for one another. One of my clients encountered this situation just recently. Among their products for sale was a legless table tray, the kind you might use to hold a dinner plate and drink in your lap while sitting on the couch or lying in bed. A competitor held a patent for a similar tray that included foldable legs. Although my client's product didn't include legs, their design was still determined to be too similar, and their product was suspended on Amazon. That presented a major problem for my client, who still had a thousand unsold trays. We approached the competitor and negotiated a six-month sell-off period, which allowed our client enough time to sell their remaining stock.

If and when you find someone infringing upon your patent, beginning with a simple cease and desist letter can be an affordable and efficient means of thwarting continued violations. If that proves unsuccessful, sellers also have the option of filing a complaint on Amazon using one of their IP infringement forms for design patents, or joining the Amazon Patent Evaluation Express (APEX), formerly known as Amazon Utility Patent Neutral Evaluation Procedure, for utility patents.

In the jurisdiction that is the Amazon universe, patent cases are a little more specialized than other IP disputes. Amazon offers sellers a neutral evaluation process that can be used to adjudicate patent disputes. There, an aggrieved utility patent holder can claim patent infringement, after which Amazon will contact the alleged offender with an email informing them they have a certain number of days to respond. Should the alleged offender do nothing, their product listing will be removed after that set number of days has expired. Should that competitor take issue with the allegations, they can also enter into APEX. Doing so requires a seller to put up a $4,000 bond, which will need to be matched by the other party in question. Thereafter, a neutral evaluator will consider the legal arguments presented by both sides and issue their ruling.

At ESQgo®, we've seen clients experience both sides of the neutral evaluation process. Recently, a client who sold clear ice molds—the kind used to make upscale ice cubes for cocktails—came to us for help after a competitor accused my client of infringing upon an existing patent. In these types of cases, there are three common defenses: first, that you are not actually infringing upon an existing patent; secondly, that an earlier court case already invalidated the patent; and finally, that there is prior artwork that would invalidate the invention. In this particular case, we went back twelve years to search for websites or other evidence that the patented product had already existed twelve plus months before the patent holder filed their patent application. We were well into that process when the patent holder dropped us from their proceedings—a lucky break. In another case, a client of ours who sold flashlights found themselves in a similar proceeding. Our historical search found prior artwork that would help our case. We discussed our findings with the opposing counsel in a well-mannered email; fourteen hours later they dropped us from their proceedings, and our client continued selling their products. (Again, the war is won or lost before it is ever fought.)

At ESQgo®, we have also represented patent holders in these disputes. One recent case involved a client who was selling a device that checked the relays of electrical components in a motor vehicle. It's a complicated piece of equipment, and one for which our client held the patent. They had found multiple sellers who were infringing upon their patent. Our client had sent cease and desist letters to these sellers, but those letters had not been heeded. We knew from past experience that the majority of alleged offenders in Amazon's neutral evaluation process either don't respond to complaints or are not willing to put up the $4,000 bond to join the program (and additional funds for attorneys). That's what happened in this case: of the eight alleged patent infringers, only one responded and joined the neutral evaluation process. And as it turned out, that seller didn't even really want to undergo the full process, they were just looking for a licensing agreement with our client that would allow them to keep selling. Our client was not willing to enter into such an agreement, and so the matter was quickly resolved in our client's favor, and the other listings were suspended.

Whether you are applying for a design, utility, or plant patent, the process is undeniably labor intensive, expensive, and lengthy. Undoubtedly, that's why many e-commerce sellers avoid it altogether. But if you are marketing a new product or one that has substantive distinctions from others on the market, that hassle and expense is probably worth it.

CHAPTER 5

Brand Enforcement

IN THE SPRING OF 2020, AS COVID-19 CASES SURGED AROUND the world, Amazon found itself battling a second epidemic: scores of listings for counterfeit N95 masks. The tight-fitting mask, which catches and filters even tiny particulates, had long been considered an essential piece of equipment for workers in industries like medicine and construction. When it was revealed that N95 masks were possibly the best defense laypeople had against the coronavirus, frenzied buyers began searching everywhere for a supply. Bad actors seized on this opportunity and began creating illegitimate product listings on Amazon, which quickly garnered tens of millions of dollars in sales and left consumers with defective or poor-quality masks.

Despite Amazon's best efforts, this epidemic of counterfeit mask sales on its marketplace continued more than a year later: in December 2021, the *New York Times* reported that counterfeit masks were still responsible for millions of dollars in sales on Amazon each month.

When it came to policing these counterfeit mask sellers, Amazon was far from alone (in fact, the gray market and black market for N95 masks became so pervasive during the pandemic that even leading hospitals fell prey). However, it is also true that the very systems and platforms that make Amazon such an appealing marketplace for legitimate sellers has also made the company particularly susceptible to counterfeits and other intellectual property violations.

According to its 2021 Brand Protection Report, Amazon successfully blocked millions of fraudulent listings and destroyed over two million counterfeit products that year alone, all part of its Brand Registry program. Founded in 2015, the registry program is Amazon's best attempt to preserve the integrity of intellectual property for its sellers. Today, over three hundred fifty thousand brands are enrolled. It's a welcomed safeguard in a world where counterfeiting and tampering is rampant, but sellers still need to be vigilant when it comes to protecting their brands and the products they sell.

Understanding the First Sale Doctrine

In Chapter 2, I briefly introduced the concept of the "gray market," which involves sellers circumventing authorized channels of distribution in order to buy and sell products at prices lower than those intended by the manufacturer. Most often, this includes purchasing a product intended for sale in one country and then reselling it in another country without the permission of the product's trademark owner (for instance, a seller might buy Sony PlayStations destined for Africa and then sell them in the United States). Doing so allows resellers to take advantage of market discrepancies, such as those seen between developing countries and more robust economies like the United States, Japan, and the United Kingdom. However, this practice also poses significant problems: not only are the products destined for these other countries often different than those sold in, say, the United States, but they may also have different packaging or warranties. More often than not, a buyer is not aware of these differences when purchasing a gray-market item, and that can lead to significant customer service problems down the road—and more importantly, a deterioration of the brand's reputation. That's one of several reasons why trademark holders can take action against gray-market sellers and prevent those sellers from hawking these goods.

Generally, once a brand owner sells its product with its trademark, the brand owner loses all right to control future sales. This is known as the *first sale doctrine*: a brand owner's trademark rights are limited to the first sale of the product. Subsequent sales of the same genuine product are beyond the scope of the brand owner's trademark rights. In other words, if I hold the trademark on Lamborghini, I can dictate how licensed dealers sell new Veneno Roadsters, but not how the people willing to pay that $6 million sticker price can resell their sports cars.

Material Difference Exception

There are two important exceptions to the first sale doctrine. The most notable of these exceptions is the concept of *material difference*. If an item being resold is *materially different* from the goods sold by the brand owner, then the reseller's products are not genuine and may constitute trademark infringement. In other words, the first sale doctrine does not apply when there's a material difference. In the case of gray-market goods, alterations to the packaging, warranties, and even the products themselves can constitute a material difference and invalidate the first sale doctrine. Other material difference exceptions to the first sale doctrine include:

- Alterations to packaging, such as the scraping of UPC codes and batch codes
- Foreign language instructions or labels
- Inferior battery life
- Different formulation of the product (i.e., when a chocolate manufacturer employs a different formula in China versus the US to match the differences in regional taste preferences)
- Expired products
- Significantly discounted price
- Unavailability of presale or postsale customer support

If goods *are* materially different, the trademark owner has several statutory remedies to either bar their importation, enjoin their sale, or seek damages for trademark infringement.

When analyzing the material difference exception, courts must first determine whether the differences between the trademark holder's goods and the unauthorized reseller's goods are "material." A difference is "material" if consumers would consider it relevant to a decision about whether to purchase a product. However, the material difference need not be physical. Rather, material differences can include nonphysical characteristics such as warranties and presale or postsale service commitments.

One of my favorite examples of postsale support is a company that sells grow-your-own-mushroom kits on Amazon. Part of the purchase price includes telephone support to help new growers troubleshoot how much to water their mushrooms or when their fungi is ready to harvest. Selling their kit without that support would most likely be a clear material difference.

One important exception to the material difference standard is refurbished goods. The material difference standard does not apply where a genuine article is used by a consumer and then refurbished and resold by a third party as "refurbished." Buyers knowingly purchasing refurbished goods do not expect the same standard of product and services as they would get with, say, a brand-new iPhone. If someone tries to sell a new iPhone on Amazon without any of the benefits offered by the manufacturer, they may be infringing upon Apple's trademark, since there is a material difference between what they are selling and what Apple offers its customers. It's a similar expectation as buying a certified used car from a dealer and receiving a limited warranty, free oil changes, and other benefits. In addition to the material difference exception to the first sale doctrine, trademark owners may also consider the quality control exception.

Quality Control Exception

Courts have developed a second exception to the first sale doctrine: the quality control exception. The exception applies when the alleged infringer "fail[s] to abide by the trademark holder's quality controls when distributing the trademarked goods or interfere[s] with the trademark holder's ability to control quality."

In other words, a trademark holder has the right to control the quality of the goods manufactured and sold under a brand's trademark. Historically, federal courts have found that goods are not considered genuine if they do not conform to the trademark holder's quality control standards. That said, for a trademark holder to seek relief for infringement under the quality control exception, they must establish that they not only maintain legitimate quality control procedures but that they also routinely abide by those procedures. Finally, they must also prove that the defendant has or will somehow diminish the value of their product and reputation through nonconforming sales.

Some quality control standards include the brand owners:

- vetting potential retailers/resellers
- monitoring authorized resellers to ensure compliance with quality control standards
- requiring retailers/resellers remove or return damaged or defective products
- having a standard operating procedure for effectively handling product recalls

- requiring retailers/resellers notify the brand about any customer complaints
- requiring their products be stored at certain storage conditions (i.e., controlled temperature/humidity)
- requiring retailers/resellers participate in the brand's rewards programs
- requiring retailers/resellers participate in brand-authorized ongoing education and training

Consider the recent case of Otter Products, a producer of cell phone and tablet cases, versus Triplenet Pricing, an online seller. Triplenet listed Otter cases on their Amazon site; included in their description of the product was Otter's limited lifetime warranty. Otter sued Triplenet, saying that Triplenet did not meet Otter's material difference and quality control standards and so could not claim a first sale doctrine defense. Specifically, Otter pointed to the detailed restrictions on how authorized dealers were required to display, ship, and report damage to Otter products. Otter also argued that the Otter products sold by Triplenet were not covered by the Otter Products warranty because Otter's warranty is limited to products purchased from the manufacturer or from an authorized seller, thereby constituting a "material difference." The court agreed and found in Otter's favor.

Enforcing Trademark Rights

A few years ago, a client came to me with a brand enforcement problem. His company had carved out a successful niche on Amazon selling hummingbird nectar and feeders. In no time, multiple other competitors were also listing identical feeders, sometimes at a fraction of the price of my client's. Most egregiously, one of these so-called competitors was actually a relative of my client's who had access to both the design schema and the tooling my client used to mass-produce his feeders. To stop his family member, my client needed to establish a material difference between his original product and the unauthorized copy being sold by his rival. We soon landed on the perfect solution: my client could begin including a small vial of their hummingbird nectar—basically, just the sugar water hummingbirds love to consume, which was only manufactured by our client—with each feeder. The vial of nectar cost next to nothing, but it gave my client an avenue to promote his full-sized nectar product and a distinct material difference, which could be used to establish material difference if his case ever went to court. Thereafter, the client updated his Amazon listing advertising this free addition to his hummingbird feeder; and we, as his attorney, sent a demand letter insisting these unauthorized sellers cease all sales of their products. Happily, they complied.

As a seller in the digital marketplace, you have a variety of strategies at your disposal for enforcing your own trademark rights. I always advise my clients to begin setting up a solid foundation long before any possible infringement has occurred. This includes, of course, applying for and securing all pertinent copyrights, trademarks, and patents. I also encourage my clients to consider offering a warranty limited to products purchased from the manufacturer or their authorized resellers, and postsale support. For instance, were my four-sided writing implement to make it to market, I might offer five years of free ink refills as part of the purchase. Because my implement is so complex in its design, I might also make it so that those refills can be made only by certified ink refillers. I could also offer a three-month warranty on my writing implements, which would further box out any would-be competitors looking to sell unauthorized versions.

Should unscrupulous individuals continue to infringe upon my trademark, my next step would probably be to send a cease and desist letter emphasizing the material difference. Each subsequent letter would become more aggressive in its language. Oftentimes, that level of action is sufficient to compel a competitor to stop abusing a brand. Of course, the more money at stake, the harder you will have to work to keep those unscrupulous sellers at bay. Sometimes, brands or businesses will need to take additional legal action, including suing a competitor in court. Trademark law does not account for mental state when determining whether or not infringement has taken place: in other words, it doesn't matter whether a defendant was knowingly infringing upon an existing trademark, or whether their actions were unintentional. However, mental state *does* come into play when a court considers damages: if a defendant is knowingly infringing upon a trademark, the plaintiff can seek (and be awarded) exponentially greater damages.

Understanding material difference and conducting a thorough material difference and quality control review is complicated work that requires a qualified attorney. In many ways, the very concept of a material difference and quality control review is still emerging law and is developing almost entirely because of the Amazon Marketplace, one more reason why hiring an IP attorney with sufficient digital commerce experience is essential. And in a world where competitors are becoming increasingly underhanded—and sophisticated in their duplicitous dealings—having an attorney skilled in the intricacies of the digital marketplace is more important than ever.

CHAPTER 6

Black Hat Tactics

IN EARLY DECEMBER 2018, AMAZON SELLERS AND CUSTOMERS alike began noticing a disturbing trend: pages maintained by reputable brands no longer featured images of the company's products. Instead, those photos had been replaced by stylized images of a Guy Fawkes mask—that narrow face distinguished by an upturned mustache and pointed goatee made popular in the *V for Vendetta* movie. Dozens—if not hundreds—of successful Amazon sellers were affected by this attack, especially those selling diet- and keto-related supplements.

Sales of these affected products plummeted (who in their right mind would buy protein powder when the image is a creepy mask?), a particularly bitter pill for those sellers, given that this was also the height of the holiday shopping season. Sellers took to an Amazon discussion board, sharing stories about how their images and listings had all been changed and, in many cases, suspended or deleted. They speculated on what had happened, and soon arrived at a theory: someone (or a group) had been selectively targeting diet and nutrition sellers and then bulk-changing their listing photos to scare away customers.

The sellers were right. This corruption of brand sites is just one of several tactics used by nefarious actors, and it is known in the world of digital marketplaces as *black hat tactics*: unscrupulous practices intended to box out or even destroy successful sellers. These techniques are most often immoral, unethical, and—most infuriatingly—not quite illegal, which makes them difficult to combat or even prevent.

Common black hat tactics involve soliciting positive reviews from customers (a practice clearly prohibited by Amazon policies) or posting fake negative reviews of competitors. Other tactics are even more sophisticated—and insidious. They include changing the descriptions of products (one black hat seller, for instance, listed cocaine as the main ingredient in his rival's multivitamins) or making unsubstantiated claims that will trigger Amazon's machine learning systems to flag or suspend a listing (another black hat seller infiltrated a rival and changed the description for carb-free pancake mix to read "this product cures cancer!").

These kinds of tactics work because of the specific nature of the contract between Amazon and its sellers. Known as the *Amazon Services Business Solutions Agreement*, or BSA for short, this contract serves as the master document governing your seller account and listings. One of the stipulations in the BSA is that Amazon can suspend or terminate your account for a variety of reasons, including deceptive, fraudulent, or illegal activity, or they feel you have engaged in any activity that might harm customers, other sellers, or what they call "Amazon's legitimate interests." This vague language gives the company great latitude when it comes to suspending or deleting listings. And black hat tacticians have found a variety of ways to exploit that latitude.

When clients come to me as the victims of black hat tactics, they are understandably confused and even angry. They don't understand how this possibly could have happened to them or how someone could have hacked their product page.

What many Amazon sellers don't understand is that their listing pages aren't actually theirs. Instead, the pages are owned by Amazon. The company's brand registry grants some control over what appears there (and who can alter that material), but a skilled black hat seller can easily infiltrate those pages and sabotage all the hard work you've done building a successful brand. In extreme cases, those same saboteurs have even contacted rival sellers on their personal cell phones and left threatening or intimidating messages.

Knowing what black hat tactics are commonly used and how you can best protect yourself is a crucial part of securing your brand.

Tactic #1: Commodifying Customer Feedback

Some of the most valuable assets an Amazon seller can have are positive product reviews—and a lot of them. So perhaps it's no surprise that unscrupulous sellers have looked for underhanded ways to enhance them. Several years ago, a common way to do that was to purchase positive reviews from fake buyer accounts whose sole purpose was to load your product listing with five-star ratings and glowing recommendations. In time, underhanded sellers realized that just as valuable as their own positive reviews were the negative ones their competitors were receiving, especially since that kind of critical feedback can really drive down a product's position in Amazon's search results. So a second cottage industry of negative product reviews quickly emerged, with participants rightly assuming that that kind of negative attention would drive would-be buyers to other products and brands.

Amazon has sought to thwart these types of sales by using artificial intelligence to monitor the rates of reviews for brands and products: if, for instance, you've averaged 10 reviews per 1,000 orders and all of a sudden you earn 100 reviews for 200 orders, that will alert the Amazon bots to note your account. Similarly, if you've made 30 sales but have received 300 reviews, that too will trigger an internal algorithm within Amazon. But part of what makes black hat tactics so difficult to police is that the people perpetrating them are constantly modifying their approach or finding ways to make it more sophisticated. That can also make it difficult to prove the reviews were generated unscrupulously and are not from actual customers.

Recently, so-called "black hatters" have also begun using these review-generating services to order hundreds or even thousands of positive reviews for their competitors' listings, knowing full well that doing so will trigger Amazon's algorithms to flag those listings as if the competitors themselves purchased the positive reviews.

Another approach to commodifying customer feedback includes offering rewards for positive reviews. Some sellers will include note cards with their products offering gift cards or an additional free product in exchange for a positive five-star review. This practice is prohibited by Amazon, but that won't prevent some of your competitors from trying it. In fact, one of my clients recently came to me with such an offer: he'd ordered a single product from one of his more successful competitors, hoping to gain some insight on what that company was selling and how they were packaging their products. Inside, he found a slip of paper offering a fifty-dollar gift card in exchange for a glowing review. On a hunch, that same client ordered similar products from several more of his competitors. They, too, included similar offers.

These were million-dollar companies that still felt the need to unfairly solicit positive feedback. (To be clear: under Amazon policy, it's fine to ask customers to leave a review, but it's not okay to ask for positive ones, or to offer any kind of compensation in exchange for those reviews.)

Tactic #2: Brushing

In many ways, the spring of 2020 was the height of the COVID-19 pandemic: our collective nerves were frayed, and the unknowability of how long lockdowns and quarantines might last had everyone on edge. Perhaps it shouldn't have been a surprise, then, that the mysterious appearance of seeds from overseas created a national uproar. Across the country, Americans reported receiving strange, unsolicited packages sent from China. Inside were unlabeled bags containing a wide range of seeds. Some individuals received hundreds of these packages, which of course intensified the alarm they were feeling. Worried calls went out to news agencies and local police departments: was this an act of bioterrorism?

An attempt to gain the mailing addresses of registered voters? Soon, elected officials and the USDA became involved. By summer's end, the latter agency had received over twenty thousand packets of seeds from concerned individuals, all of whom swore the packages were unsolicited and not from any foreign person or company they knew or recognized.

It didn't take long before digital market insiders began to suspect that these seeds were part of an elaborate black hat campaign from a foreign Amazon seller. Known as "brushing," this tactic involves sellers sending unsolicited packages containing nearly worthless items, such as a single hair band, a cheap plastic toy, or even a package of seeds to a random individual or home address. Basically, a black hatter or a group of black hatters will create hundreds of fake Amazon buyer accounts; these fake buyer accounts will be used to place orders for a specific product the group is trying to promote. When these bogus Amazon buyer accounts place the orders on Amazon, they are training Amazon's algorithm that this specific product sells well and therefore should be promoted to the top of the search results for such a search term. The black hatters, in return, send worthless products to these random addresses to save on shipping and product costs instead of sending their own valuable product. Doing so allows a fake buyer account to input the tracking information for the worthless item into Amazon's system. That tracking information validates the so-called sale and makes it appear as if the sale was conducted effectively and the items were delivered on time. It also allows the black hatter who sent the unsolicited item to then go in and give themselves a glowing, five-star review that won't be flagged by an Amazon bot. The proliferation of both stolen credit card information and untraceable virtual credit cards (known in the industry as "brick" cards) makes it all but impossible for Amazon to track down who is responsible for a brushing campaign.

It's still not clear whether or not that's what was happening with the thousands of packets of seeds arriving in the US during the summer of 2020. Some buyers swear they were being brushed. A July 2021 *Atlantic* article investigated the claims and found that, at least in some cases, buyers actually purchased seeds but didn't realize they'd be coming from China (and that huge shipping delays exacerbated by the pandemic would mean they received the seeds months after they ordered them). Regardless of what was afoot in this particular instance, the brushing phenomenon is certainly alive and well in today's digital marketplace. And the fact remains that there are also plenty of people who, upon receiving an Amazon box with an item they didn't order or pay for are more than happy to write a glowing review for the free coffee mug or cutting board they found inside.

Tactic #3: Spending Your Money

There's nothing a nefarious seller loves more than costing you business and profits, and many will go to surprising ends to do just that. The advertising model at Amazon is a click-and-pay one: in other words, if you choose to make one of your products a sponsored one, you only pay when a potential customer clicks on your product's advertisement. Knowing this, black hatters can now utilize bots that continuously click on their competitors' ads, driving up their advertising bills.

Another tactic is to purchase dozens of your products, only to return them. Not only does this wipe you out of inventory at a crucial time and prevent you from selling to others, but it also gives the black hatter the opportunity to write a verified negative review of you and your product. And even if the black hatter returns your inventory in good condition, you are still out a considerable amount of money, particularly if you are using Fulfillment by Amazon. On average, Amazon keeps about 25 percent of all FBA sales. The online giant may refund a small portion of that percentage if an item is returned, but the bulk will still be retained. And if a black hatter returns your inventory with even minor damage (such as a ding to the product's box), you will only be able to sell that item as used, which can drop your profit margin on the item to nearly zero.

Tactic #4: Bogus IP Complaints

Some black hatters will also file false intellectual property complaints just to gum up your schedule with unnecessary correspondence and even the need to hire legal representation. Consider one of our clients, who sold religious items like crosses, rugs, and photographs imported from Mexico. Out of the blue, our client began receiving repeated complaints that they were infringing upon other sellers' copyrights. Their product listings were then suspended by Amazon. We could tell that these claims were bogus and most likely from my client's main competitors, so we filed a counternotice denying the claims. Amazon's policy, per the Digital Millennium Copyright Act (DMCA), is to give a complainant ten days to consider this counternotice and to decide if they want to sue before Amazon lifts a suspension. My client's competitor had no intention of pursuing a lawsuit, but they knew those ten days would result in lost revenue for my client and the opportunity for the competitor to build a stronger customer base. Not only that, but the black hat competitor also knew they could launch another ten-day suspension as soon as one ended.

Luckily for my client, we could see what their nefarious competitor was up to. We contacted Amazon's attorneys and provided evidence of this black hat tactic. The attorneys agreed with our interpretation of what was happening and suspended the competitor's ability to file IP complaints against our client. We assumed the case was closed and that our client had been handed a total victory until the complaints started up again a few weeks later: turns out, our client's competitor had enlisted his mother-in-law to file the complaints. We had her blocked as well, but the complaints kept coming. Soon it became clear that this competitor had enlisted other friends and members of his family to lodge complaints as well. In the end, our client was forced to file a lawsuit against the competitor. All along, he had only wanted to play by Amazon's rules, but his competitor had found a way to use those rules to an unfair advantage.

Illegal Tactics: Exploiting Insider Know-How

In 2020, the United States Department of Justice announced that it had indicted six people for allegedly conspiring to bribe Amazon employees. The six individuals, who hailed from the US and India, were accused of participating in a $100 million bribery scheme that also involved at least ten Amazon employees. In exchange for these bribes, the accused had allegedly reactivated suspended accounts, suspended seller accounts of competitors, and negative reviews removed from their pages. The sheer amount of money and scope of this bribery scandal made it international news for days, but this was far from the only instance of such tactics.

Just recently, I received an email from an individual saying that they could provide insider information about my clients' account health, including internal notes about those accounts made by internal Amazon staff members. These kinds of solicitations are becoming all too common. Most come from anonymous providers hiding behind websites pretending to offer legitimate services. Instead, they are created and maintained by individuals who have obtained information through illegal or immoral means, including bribery or unscrupulous family members stealing or logging into employees' accounts. I've yet to see a legitimate (or even legal) offer of this kind, so my personal response is always to send those offers directly to the Amazon attorneys.

What to Do as a Black Hat Victim

Amazon's Business Solutions Agreement stipulates that it will notify any seller of a suspension or termination, along with any options you may have for an appeal. One exception to that rule is if providing that information to a seller may hinder an investigation or allow sellers to circumvent safeguards. What that means is that, if black hat tactics have created the appearance that you are perpetrating fraud, you may not know the details or even the reasons behind your suspension until Amazon has completed its investigation—if ever.

The unfortunate truth is that there isn't a lot you *can* do when you've become the victim of black hat tactics (just ask those supplement companies who lost thousands of dollars in revenue when their products were replaced with Guy Fawkes masks back in 2018). But that doesn't mean you can't do your due diligence from the start. I always advise my clients to keep a detailed paper trail from the moment they suspect they have become victims. This can include taking screenshots of listings that have been tampered with, preserving correspondences, or anything else that might demonstrate someone has unfairly manipulated your listings.

Don't assume that your account may be suspended or terminated if and when black hat tactics occur. However, if you do notice any irregularities, it's best to notify Amazon immediately and create a paper trail. In that case, your best course of action is to create a case with Amazon's Seller Central, the backend portal for Amazon sellers. There, you can create a claims ticket notifying Amazon of what has occurred. When creating such a ticket, always stick to specific facts, including the dates and times of a violation, as well as the nature of the tactic used against you. If this is your first time creating such a claim, it's often a good idea to have a friend, family member, or colleague read your narrative to help you evaluate if you've provided enough detail and evidence to make your case clear.

Certainly there are times when it is worth pursuing more formal legal action, but you always need to conduct your own cost–benefit analysis: is it worth hiring an attorney to take it to Amazon's legal team? If you're sitting on at least $10,000 worth of inventory, it may be. If you're selling $500 worth of handmade soap per year, it may not. Be sure to work with your attorney to develop your own cost–benefit analysis, which should include the number of units in your possession and the future outlook of your products. If you are talking about less than $10,000 in annual revenue, chances are a case isn't going to be cost effective, even if you are completely in the right. Consider one of my clients, who sold supplements on Amazon. His arch competitor had begun paying friends and family members to purchase my client's products and leave negative reviews. Using social media, we could trace the author of these reviews back to my client's competitor (all of the reviewers, for instance, were friends of the competitor on Facebook). We went to Amazon with our complaint and evidence of these social connections, only to be told by Amazon's attorneys that they didn't have enough evidence to make a judgment. So my client opted to hire a private investigator. Under the guise of planning a surprise retirement party for my client's competitor, the private investigator began calling the individuals who had left reviews. Using that simple ruse, the investigator was able to establish that all of the individuals leaving the negative reviews were friends of the competitors, and in many cases, he was able to get those individuals to admit what they had been doing, all the while having no idea that they were talking to a PI hired by my client. The recordings of those conversations (and confessions) led to a huge settlement for my client—but they were also very expensive to obtain.

A stubborn or sophisticated competitor will adjust and evolve their methods, making it difficult to shut them down entirely. Sometimes, as was the case with my client who imported Mexican religious items, the only option available to you is an expensive lawsuit. That kind of legal action is too cost prohibitive for many sellers, which is cold comfort, I know. If you're one of them, you can at least take solace in the knowledge that black hatters only target serious competitors. In other words, if you've become the victim of black hat tactics, it's because you've become a serious seller who has entered the big leagues. That won't help you prevent the black hat tactics from happening, but it does mean you've done a great job of building a successful digital marketplace.

CHAPTER 7

Standing Up to the Giant

THOSE SAME AMAZON ALGORITHMS INTENDED TO PROTECT
you from black hat tactics can also hamper your success.
Just how much damage can they do? Ask one of my clients
who made the kind of news no seller wants back in 2020,
when Amazon destroyed about $1.5 million worth of his
merchandise.

Here's how it happened. For years, my client ran a successful
high-end clothing store in Los Angeles. As the COVID-
19 pandemic swept across the nation, my client made the
decision to close his LA store and sell the apparel exclusively
online, using the features offered by Fulfillment by Amazon.
That decision also meant he had to ship the entirety of his

inventory (over $1 million worth of clothes) to Amazon, which in turn distributed it to several of its warehouses around the country.

As far as my client could tell, the decision was initially a profitable one: he began receiving a steady stream of orders, and customer reviews were positive. But then, just a few short months later, he received notification that his account was under review. Apparently, four of his customers had contacted Amazon complaining about the condition of the products they received and suggesting that they were counterfeit.

With that notification, my client found himself immersed in the lengthy, byzantine, and sometimes utterly frustrating world of Amazon's appeals process. He tried providing invoices proving that the clothes he was selling were from legitimate brands, but Amazon refused to consider the invoices, noting that those documents were over a year old. (The invoices accurately represented the date when my client purchased the goods; he had been storing them in his own warehouse since then.) Amazon warned my client that it was preparing to destroy his inventory, but then sent a series of conflicting dates as to when that would happen and what his deadline was to appeal the decision. He tried contacting Amazon's C-suite directly, but a spokesperson told him there was nothing more to be done. Nearly his entire inventory was destroyed shortly thereafter—as was his career and his life's savings.

I wish I could say that my client's experience with Amazon was highly extraordinary. Unfortunately, it's not. In fact, a House Judiciary Committee report issued in 2020 found that digital marketplaces like Amazon mistreat their sellers far too often. Knowing how to respond is almost always your best defense.

Friend or Foe?

That same House Judiciary Committee report highlighted several key ways sellers are potentially underserved—if not entirely undermined—by digital marketplaces like Amazon. Publicly, Amazon refers to you as a "third-party seller." Internally, you are known as a "competitor." To my mind, this is no mere semantic distinction. Instead, it calls attention to the complicated relationships and conflicting interests inherent on the platform (even the House committee saw this distinction as a conflict of interest), which often do not serve third-party sellers.

Recall that Amazon has its own internal brands, which are developed and curated by brand managers. One category overseen by these brand managers might be kitchen supplies. That kitchen supplies manager may be responsible for generating, say, $25 million annually in kitchen gadgets and cookware. That person is understandably going to look for ways to build profitability for the Amazon brand, especially where new products are concerned. A perfect place to look is at what items are selling particularly well on the Amazon site. If it happens to be your bamboo cutting boards or garlic press, you can understand how easy and appealing it might be for that brand manager to begin manufacturing and selling your products under the Amazon label—since that brand manager has access to Amazon-proprietary data, and can identify the sales data for each third-party product listed on the site.

That same brand manager might also be inclined to read the reviews for your product. Maybe, for instance, customers complain that your cutting boards aren't dishwasher safe or your garlic press needs to be a hair bigger to accommodate an average-sized garlic clove. Because of its scale, Amazon can easily exploit its economies of scale to make these design tweaks and begin selling an improved version of your product in no time. And because Amazon has all of the data behind your sales, it's that much easier for them to compete.

Since its inception, Amazon has been focused on cost-cutting strategies, which is one reason why it's so easy for them to make your product better and sell it for less money. Those strategies have also been behind Amazon's emphasis on automated processes in nearly every aspect of the company. And while Amazon has spent significant amounts of money and resources on customer service for buyers, one place it has scrimped is similar services for its sellers—another shortcoming emphasized by that House committee report (in their defense, Amazon executives argued that they only utilize "aggregate data," or data anonymized because it comes from multiple sellers, but they were also evasive about just how large—or small—these pools of aggregate data really are).

That same House committee report found that Amazon has repeatedly used its own brand standard policies to force third-party sellers into wholesale relationships with Amazon or to shut down these sellers entirely. It also found evidence that the online giant has wrongly forced third-party sellers to submit sensitive information, including authentic invoices, which in turn allows Amazon to set its own, more competitive prices. The House committee report also states that Amazon gives its own listings preferential treatment, pointing customers to their offerings before directing would-be customers to a third-party listing.

This kind of self-reflexive preferential treatment reached a particularly pernicious level during the COVID-19 pandemic, when Amazon announced that it would delay the delivery of all nonessential shipments in order to "protect" its warehouse workers. What they didn't announce was that the company exempted its own products from this nonessential designation. In other words: Amazon delayed the delivery of all third-party so-called nonessential items while continuing to sell and deliver similar products sold by Amazon directly.

Responding to a Suspension Notification

Amazon has always been veiled about how it determines which sellers they have suspended and why, often citing proprietary algorithms as the driving determiner. What they do reveal is that suspensions on digital marketplaces like Amazon can happen for a variety of reasons, including perceived intellectual property infringement. Many of these cases are not clear cut, which is another reason why it's worth retaining a good IP attorney. Take the case of one of my clients, who sold canvas wheel covers for sport utility vehicles. His logo included the letter J, followed by two dog paw prints, followed by the letter P. Was this a trademark infringement on Jeep? Amazon thought so and suspended his product listing (or ASIN—Amazon Standard Identification Number —a unique set of ten numbers and letters that identifies each product on the site). However, I saw a case to be made that the two logos were not, in fact, confusingly similar.

Another client sold T-shirts emblazoned with a skull that resembled the Marvel comic character Punisher. He, too, was suspended. That case raises the question of how similar is too similar. Certainly a case could be made that most people—especially comic fans—could distinguish between what my client was selling and what Marvel had copyrighted. In the case of my client's skull art, the jawline, teeth, and eye sockets were clearly different—but not different enough, according to Amazon.

In cases like these, Amazon has the option of merely suspending or deactivating a single listing, rather than an entire seller account. In fact, the company has made good progress in recent years establishing different levels and categories for suspensions. Some are performance based (you don't ship your products out on time, you consistently receive negative reviews, you're not uploading your tracking information). Others are for IP violations, such as those above.

Regardless of why you are suspended, it's important to keep in mind that, in the sovereign nation that is Amazon, you are guilty until proven innocent. Also, the burden for proving infringement is quite low, which also leaves you vulnerable to such accusations.

In the last chapter, I told you that Amazon is not required to notify a seller why they are being suspended if the company determines that doing so may either hinder an investigation or do harm. While that's true, Amazon most often does notify sellers why they are being suspended, at least in broad terms. In order to appeal that decision, a seller must provide Amazon with a *plan of action* (or POA), such as the following:

Dear Seller Performance:

I am the principal of ▓▓▓▓▓▓▓▓▓▓▓ a.k.a. ▓▓▓▓▓▓▓▓▓▓▓ and I am writing to appeal the suspension of our account due to inauthentic product complaints for ASIN ▓▓▓▓▓▓ and ▓▓▓▓▓▓▓. We understand that Amazon takes these complaints seriously so we have thoroughly examined our account to determine the root cause of the issue and implemented appropriate remedies.

INVOICES

- The products we sold under ASIN ▓▓▓▓▓▓ and ▓▓▓▓▓▓ C were sourced from ▓▓▓▓▓▓▓▓▓▓▓▓▓▓▓▓▓▓▓▓▓▓▓▓. We submitted a copy of our invoice twice in our previous submissions and it was rejected by Seller Performance twice. Because of this, we are now attaching a letter from the supplier confirming that we have ceased all business with them.

ROOT CAUSE

- We failed to verify if this supplier was an authorized distributor of ▓▓▓▓▓▓ products before sourcing these products from them. Therefore, when we received multiple complaints that the product was defective, ineffective or not as described, we had no document to support that these products were authentic.

ACTIONS TAKEN TO RESOLVE THE ISSUE

- We terminated our relationship with ▓▓▓▓▓▓▓▓▓▓▓, and we will not source any products from them again. Please see the attached communication as proof of this action.

- We will permanently stop selling ▓▓▓▓▓ products on the Amazon marketplace.

- We will not source these products/ASINs from any other suppliers.

STEPS TO PREVENT THE ISSUE GOING FORWARD

- We carefully reviewed all our other suppliers and requested supply chain documentation from them to ensure that the products we sell on the Amazon Marketplace are authentic.

- We deleted all product listings for items sourced from ▓▓▓▓▓▓▓▓▓ and any other supplier that could not provide us with supply chain documentation.

- We reviewed relevant Amazon policies, particularly:
  - Product Detail Page Rules
    (https://sellercentral.amazon.com/gp/help/200390640)
  - Condition guidelines
    (https://sellercentral.amazon.com/gp/help/200339950)
  - Amazon Product Authenticity and Quality
    (https://sellercentral.amazon.com/gp/help/G202010130)
  - and Prohibited Seller Activities and Actions
    (https://sellercentral.amazon.com/gp/help/200386250)

- Moving forward, we will only source products from authorized distributors and/or directly from the manufacturer so that we have invoices to support the authenticity of all our products. This will prevent inauthentic product complaints in the future.

Sincerely,

The first section of a POA such as this one includes an outline of the root cause (the reason why you were suspended). Obviously, this can be difficult to describe if Amazon has been broad or even vague in its description of your suspension. That can leave sellers in the position of having to guess about the nature of their suspension; guessing incorrectly will delay the process even further and can cost you valuable sales. Next, the second section of a POA includes immediate steps the third party has implemented to prevent this issue from recurring. Finally, the third section of a POA describes the changes in the business practice that have been completed to prevent this issue from recurring.

Whenever a client comes to ESQgo® with a suspension, the first thing my team and I do is to collect information about the case, which allows us to conduct a thorough legal analysis. Our primary aim is to consider the facts of the case against Amazon's policies in order to determine what policy, if any, was violated by our client and whether or not Amazon was acting reasonably when it issued the suspension. Only then will we prepare a plan of action such as the one above.

Most often, the Amazon representatives who review POAs are not trained attorneys, nor do they have backgrounds in IP law, so it's always useful to keep the documents brief and as straightforward as possible. It's also worth noting that the approval process can be highly subjective: I've had clients who have submitted POAs that have been rejected, only to have the exact same POA accepted when it was resubmitted.

If a POA is rejected by Amazon, the next step we will take is to contact Amazon's Account Health Department, which can help guide a seller about how to revise a rejected POA or what, specifically, that original document lacked. Knowing that this is an available option, we also conclude each POA by asking its reviewer to make notes about any potential rejection in their internal system. Those kinds of notes are what allow the Account Health Department to assess a rejected POA and offer valuable feedback about how to rectify any shortcomings or problems it may have before resubmitting the document.

If a POA is again rejected by Amazon, a seller still has additional recourse, including sending a letter to Amazon's legal team or their Escalations Department. If neither of those correspondences yield any positive action, a seller can also send a letter directly to the email address of its founder, Jeff Bezos. Obviously, Mr. Bezos doesn't read these letters, but they do often find their way to his executive team, who can investigate a case. If that still doesn't work, a client can also file a complaint with the Better Business Bureau, who in turn can contact Amazon on the client's behalf. A seller also has the option of taking Amazon to small claims court. States and even counties vary in terms of the maximum compensation that can be sought there (here in LA County, a corporation cannot sue for more than $5,000, which is just a tiny fraction of what most of our clients lost).

Regardless which venue you choose, be prepared for a long ride. Depending upon how complex your case is, it can take your own legal counsel up to a week to prepare your response to Amazon. Their attorneys, in turn, may take weeks to investigate your claim.

Many of my clients understandably want to know why they need to complete a plan of action. Amazon has never made its reasoning for this three-part document public, but I have a theory.

From a legal perspective, acknowledging the root cause is tantamount to admitting guilt and assuming responsibility for any wrongdoing. I suspect that requiring such a statement is one way Amazon attempts to protect itself if for any reason the matter goes to litigation or arbitration. For that reason, and because they can be subpoenaed, I always caution clients to consider any POA a public document and to choose their words very carefully. An IP law attorney will understand the weight of vocabulary and how best to craft a document that won't later damage your reputation (for instance, I always avoid using words like "breached" or "infringed": both are legal words that come with a lot more weight than most laypeople realize). Finding that balance between taking responsibility and incriminating yourself is difficult.

As is the case with much of the internet, Amazon's policies are always changing. Even a law firm specializing in IP and digital sales has difficulty keeping up with these changes (there are even entire Facebook groups dedicated to single topics like Amazon suspension policies). Staying informed is always the first step in reversing any potential suspension.

Ask most sellers who have been suspended, and they'll tell you they feel like they have no choice but to return to the Amazon Marketplace as soon as possible, no matter how badly they feel like they've been treated—partly because there isn't another feasible alternative to Amazon. That's just one more reason why sellers need effective means of confronting the digital giant when they feel that they have been wrongly accused or suspended. At ESQgo®, we've developed just the solution, which I explain in detail in the next chapter.

CHAPTER 8

Synthetic Arbitration®

RECALL FROM THE LAST CHAPTER THE CASE OF MY CLIENT whose inventory was destroyed by Amazon after several customers claimed it was counterfeit. Obviously, there was nothing we could do to restore my client's merchandise—or his listings on Amazon. The only recourse that remained was to seek damages.

If you find yourself in a similar situation where Amazon is responsible or at fault, the first question to ask yourself is how best to ascertain the value of your loss and what might be considered a reasonable sum as compensation. Given how quickly legal fees amass, it's often not financially advisable to pursue a legal case if your losses are under $150,000, since it could easily cost upwards of $80,000 to litigate a case in arbitration before the American Arbitration Association (AAA).

Amazon's Business Solutions Agreement (BSA) is structured such that sellers can pursue arbitration. Unlike mediation, where two sides come together in the hopes of arriving at a mutually agreed upon compromise or solution, arbitration works similar to a court insofar as the arbitrator makes a binding ruling after hearing both sides. This approach has obvious benefits for Amazon: whereas court documents are public, arbitration proceedings are confidential, which means that other sellers cannot see the outcome of your proceedings. Amazon also employs a lone law firm for almost all of its arbitration cases, which means they can track the cases as well as how different arbitrators decide. Sellers, on the other hand, only have access to the cases pursued by their legal counselor—just a piece of the pie that Amazon has in its entirety. Undoubtedly, that inside track is one reason why, over the past five years, only a very tiny fraction of third-party sellers pursued arbitration with Amazon. In fact, the US Senate found that only 0.008 percent of Amazon sellers have ever engaged in arbitration with the online giant. And while the number of those sellers continues to increase dramatically, that infinitesimal percentage has remained nearly constant.

One major reason for that tiny number is because of the cost of arbitration. Even small-scale Amazon sellers can expect to spend about $80,000 on an arbitration case. Those that can afford such an expensive legal fee will still face a long and often uphill battle.

As the following graphic demonstrates, arbitration is also a long and complicated process.

ARBITRATION ROADMAP

FILING & INITIATION
Day 1-15

(BSA Prerequisite) Send a letter requesting arbitration and describing your claim to Amazon's registered agent.

Thereafter, an Amazon Seller submits a Demand for Arbitration, a copy of the BSA, and the appropriate filing fee to the AAA.

EXPECTED COSTS
+ AAA Admin Fees
+ Attorney Fees

ARBITRATOR SELECTION
Day 15-44

AAA identifies arbitrators from the AAA National Roster of Arbitrators and provides their curriculum vitae to the parties.

The AAA invites the most mutually agreeable arbitrator(s) to serve on the case.

EXPECTED COSTS
+ AAA Admin Fees
+ Attorney Fees

PRELIMINARY HEARING
Day 44-85

Parties and arbitrator discuss the substantive issues of the case and procedural matters, such as discovery, witness lists, and dates.

The Scheduling Order, which serves as the framework for hearing preparations, is established.

EXPECTED COSTS
+ AAA Admin Fees
+ Attorney Fees

DISCOVERY
Day 85-222

The parties work within the time frames set forth at the Preliminary Hearing to exchange information and prepare their presentations. The arbitrator addresses any challenges related to information sharing.

EXPECTED COSTS
+ AAA Admin Fees
+ Attorney Fees

EVIDENTIARY HEARING
Day 222-258

Parties present testimony and evidence to the arbitrator.

EXPECTED COSTS
+ AAA Admin Fees
+ Attorney Fees

POST-HEARING DOCS/AWARD
Day 258-288

If the arbitrator allows, parties may submit additional documentation. The arbitrator closes the record and, no more than thirty days later, issues a decision addressing all claims raised in the arbitration. completed when the award is issued.

EXPECTED COSTS
+ AAA Admin Fees
+ Attorney Fees
+ Arbitrator Fees

As you can see, it's a labor-intensive process that requires a substantial amount of research. It's also a highly subjective process. Arbitrators try to be fair, but they are, of course, human and arrive with their own subjectivities and even biases. Some arbitrators may be stricter than others about what can be included or even show their hand with regards to how they feel about Amazon's business process.

The actual arbitration evidentiary hearing can take as little as a few hours or as long as a week. During that time, both sides have the opportunity to present their evidence, along with testimony from any witnesses. After the hearing, the arbitrator may also request additional information or documents to help them make their decision. Those decisions can be delivered one of two ways: *reasoned,* in which case the arbitrator provides an explanation or justification for their ruling, or *unreasoned*, in which case the arbitrator merely provides their decision. In either case, the entire arbitration process can sometimes take as long as a year or more. Depending upon what brought you to arbitration in the first place, that could mean your business's Amazon account is suspended the entire time, which could easily become a financial death knell for a company

—especially when you have no revenue or profit but still must pay for the attorney fees, AAA filing fees, and arbitrator fees.

That's precisely why we at ESQgo® created Synthetic Arbitration®, or SynArb®. Designed with the best interest of both sellers and Amazon in mind, SynArb® offers sellers a streamlined way to seek a remedy from Amazon. Not only does this process take half the time of formal arbitration, it also costs just a fraction of the price.

The SynArb® Process

Several years ago, a new client came to us with a very expensive problem. In preparation for the launch of twenty-five new products, our client attempted to use one of the one hundred thousand UPC codes she had purchased years ago. However, when the client went to enter these codes into Amazon, she discovered that the codes had already been claimed by another seller who was listing completely different types of products. Apparently, a bad actor had found a block of UPC codes not currently in circulation and had sold them illegally. By the time my client realized this, the bad actor had issued them to other sellers. Consequently, my client was left with a warehouse of new products and no way to sell them. The client could have pursued arbitration, but not only would the cost of such a process have ruined her business, it also would have prevented our client from selling any of her products for months—or even longer. Purchasing new codes and replacing the existing packaging was also going to cost our client several hundred thousand dollars and a lot of time since she would need to reprint thousands of boxes with new UPC codes. Either way, this small business was going to be stuck—if not altogether sunk.

Instead, through the SynArb® process, we were able to offer that client a viable option and the prospect of immediate action. We contacted Amazon's attorneys and explained the situation and how our client had been unfairly victimized. Due to the huge undertaking of having to unlink about eighty thousand unauthorized UPC codes from listings across several countries (Amazon marketplaces); Amazon estimated that it would take several months. Instead, we worked with Amazon's attorneys to clear twenty-five UPC codes already imprinted on our client's new-to-be-launched products, while Amazon's attorneys worked tirelessly to resolve the issues with the remaining UPC codes. That allowed our client to continue launching her new products while Amazon conducted their investigation into the other stolen codes.

SynArb® for Libelous Competitor Attacks

Using this proprietary process, we represented a client who had been maliciously attacked by a competitor who posed as a buyer and left a libelous negative product review on their listing. Specifically, our client was marketing over-the-counter health supplements. Their competitor erroneously alleged that some of our client's products contained ingredients included on the FDA recall list, a false and deliberately libelous claim. In a firm, well-reasoned letter, we brought this issue before Amazon's legal counsel and demanded that Amazon remove the libelous content and investigate potential violations of customer product reviews policies. After a few back-and-forth communications with Amazon's attorneys, the libelous negative product review was successfully removed from our client's listing.

SynArb® for Lost or Destroyed FBA Inventory

We've used SynArb® to help clients get reimbursed for lost or damaged inventory that was stored at FBA. We've been able to help sellers get reimbursements from $20,000 to nearly $2 million. In one particular case, Amazon's fulfillment centers lost $1.8 million of our client's inventory—an inconceivable amount of products in any world except for Amazon's, where hundreds of millions of products move through FBA centers each year. As if this weren't bad enough, our client's correspondence with Amazon initially went unanswered; when we were finally able to get a response from the e-commerce giant, they didn't even have enough information about the lost products to investigate internally. Using SynArb®, we were able to negotiate a fair settlement for our client.

SynArb® for Stranded Inventory

Unlike lost or stolen inventory, stranded items are those that have either been miscategorized or gone unlisted. In other words, Amazon knows exactly where the inventory is located, but listings for those items have either been frozen or never existed in the first place. As a result, the products languish in an FBA warehouse, and neither the seller nor potential buyer can access them. A few years ago, a client of mine listed a new brand of paintball guns and pellets on their seller site. Amazon's AI cataloging services wrongly flagged the products as dangerous (Amazon prohibits the sale of ammunition), and so the inventory was never even listed on the seller's page and, instead, languished in a fulfillment center. Our client had tried repeatedly to contact the appropriate Amazon offices and explain the mistake, but to no avail. Without SynArb®, that client would have been forced to either surrender thousands of dollars of goods or undergo a lengthy arbitration process that may well have cost more than the paintball guns and pellets were worth. With SynArb®, we were able to fast-track the case and work with Amazon to rectify the mistake. Within weeks, our client's paintball products were actively listed and enjoying brisk sales.

SynArb® for Internal Business Conflict

Disputes between business partners are inevitable. Left unresolved, a partnership dispute can lead to lost profits and an implosion of the business. This happened to one of our clients, who came to us for help with his Amazon Seller account suspension and over $300,000 worth of funds withheld by Amazon.

Our client built a thriving Amazon business as a solo entrepreneur for several years before making the decision to welcome partners. When the partnership was formed, our client updated all relevant information in Seller Central to reflect the new partnership's email address, legal entity, and bank information. Everything was going well for the first few months of the new partnership until their seller account was suspended for "not fulfilling orders after confirming shipments." Our client soon determined that the new partners were at fault and terminated the relationship. Our client also decided to revert information on the seller account back to the original email address, company information, and bank account. This ultimately caused the account to be flagged by Amazon for suspicious activity and possible fraud, thereby causing all parties to lose access to Seller Central. It was messy!

Thankfully, our client and his partners agreed to settle their dispute amicably. And using our proprietary Synthetic

Arbitration® process, we brought their seller account issues before Amazon's attorneys. In a firm, well-reasoned letter, we explained the facts of the case and demanded that Amazon promptly release our client's sales proceeds, grant them access to Seller Central, and reinstate selling privileges. After completing their own investigation, Amazon found that our client's claims had merit, and they granted our client all the reliefs we demanded.

SynArb® for Rogue Employees

Our team was hired to help reinstate and gain back control over an Amazon Seller account that had been hijacked by a rogue employee. Our client had made the unfortunate mistake of trusting a treacherous employee with full control over their Amazon Seller account. Without our client's knowledge and permission, that employee changed the primary email address on the account and thereafter changed the bank account for the deposit method in Seller Central.

Using our proprietary Synthetic Arbitration® process, we brought this issue before Amazon's legal team. After a few back-and-forth communications with Amazon's attorneys, our client finally gained back full control of their Amazon Seller account and had the rogue employee booted from their account.

SynArb® for External Tampering

We've also had situations where a client's competitor has gained access to our client's brand registry accounts and used that access to file erroneous complaints. In another instance, my client learned that their supplier had begun manufacturing my client's products on their own and selling them directly to Amazon. In this case, Amazon was not the offending party, but SynArb® still led to a successful outcome because we were able to prove that our client was the rightful trademark holder.

Conclusion

TO DATE, ESQGO® HAS INITIATED OVER 250 SYNARB® CASES.
They work because they consistently benefit both the seller
and Amazon. We know that we are serving our clients well
and that their potential for success is high. Our SynArb® process has given ESQgo® a clear competitive advantage, which
is one reason why other IP attorneys refer their clients to
us. Since its founding, ESQgo® has had a vision and mission
of developing solutions that are both creative and logical
and that benefit the online selling community. We provide
much-needed reliability and predictability in the frontier
space that is the world of Amazon. As more and more companies enter the digital marketplace and independent delivery
stream, these tools will become increasingly useful for sellers
of all stripes.

The digital marketplace continues to grow and change. It may soon be the case that sellers are able to sue Amazon directly, which will open yet another legal venue to pursue. In the meantime, knowing your arbitration responsibilities, as spelled out in the BSA, and the opportunities afforded by SynArb® will help ensure you are treated fairly as a third-party seller.

Amazon is far from a perfect company, concept, or marketplace. There's a lot that still needs to be improved on all three fronts. At ESQgo®, we tend to see the worst of this world, whether it's underhanded tactics by malevolent competitors or bureaucratic logjams created by Amazon itself. It's not uncommon for one of my clients, at the height of their frustration, to disavow Amazon and swear they'll never return to the marketplace. In my experience, they almost always change their minds. For the foreseeable future, Amazon really is the main game in town, and if you want to sell online, there are few other viable options.

I also want to make clear that both I and the rest of my firm continue to believe not only in the potential of e-commerce, but also the current opportunities that exist at sites like

Amazon. Already, there is a vibrant community of small and medium sellers who have made millions of dollars and changed their families' lives for the better. Yes, some important changes need to be made: we would all benefit if Amazon had more competition, if there was greater transparency for both buyers and sellers, and if policies were created that really were in the best interest of both contingents. I would like to see a day in the not-too-distant future when Amazon sellers were considered innocent until proven guilty and the internal legal processes more closely resembled those of the US legal and court systems. Together, we can work to compel Amazon to make those changes. And, in the meantime, ESQgo® will be here, ready to help if and when you find yourself on the wrong side of an Amazon dispute.